“十四五”职业教育国家规划教材

U0756077

普通高等学校小学教育专业系列教材

小学英语教学技能实训

主　编　朱　莹

副主编　杨　璐

编　委　管　玲　顾　振　徐荣荣　谢　清　王　冠

　　　　韩莉莉　乔　炜　王长河

复旦大学出版社

复旦学前云平台
数字化教学支持说明

为提高教学服务水平，促进课程立体化建设，复旦大学出版社学前教育分社建设了"复旦学前云平台"，为师生提供丰富的课程配套资源，可通过"电脑端"和"手机端"查看、获取。

【电脑端】

电脑端资源包括 PPT 课件、电子教案、习题答案、课程大纲、音频、视频等内容。可登录"复旦学前云平台"www.fudanxueqian.com 浏览、下载。

Step 1 登录网站"复旦学前云平台"www.fudanxueqian.com，点击右上角"登录 / 注册"，使用手机号注册。

Step 2 在"搜索"栏输入相关书名，找到该书，点击进入。

Step 3 点击【配套资源】中的"下载"（首次使用需输入教师信息），即可下载。音频、视频内容可通过搜索该书【视听包】在线浏览。

📱【手机端】

PPT 课件、音视频、阅读材料：用微信扫描书中二维码即可浏览。

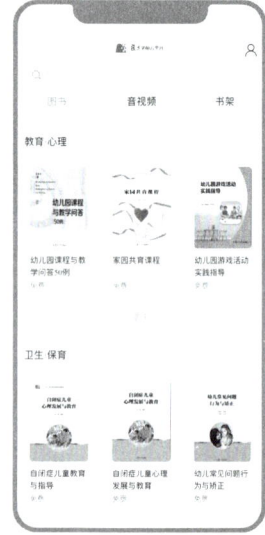
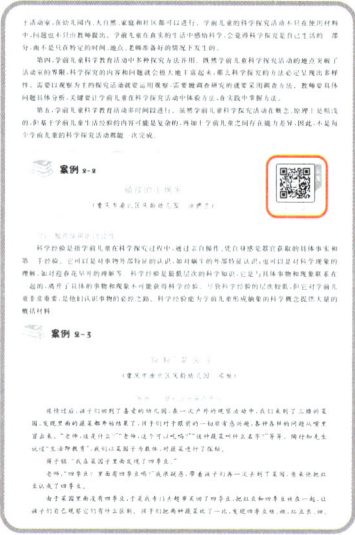

📖【更多相关资源】

更多资源，如专家文章、活动设计案例、绘本阅读、环境创设、图书信息等，可关注"幼师宝"微信公众号，搜索、查阅。

平台技术支持热线：029-68518879。

"幼师宝"微信公众号

前　言

　　《小学英语教学技能实训》紧密围绕党的二十大报告最新精神,坚持立德树人根本任务,秉持"价值观塑造、能力锻造、人格养成、知识传递"理念,在教学内容中嵌入关爱学生、教书育人等职业道德规范和科学的教育理念,注重以人为本、因材施教,注重学用相长、知行合一,培养教育情怀,提升教师职业道德,引导学生树立正确的世界观、人生观、价值观,旨在使学生习得专业知识与树立正确、崇高的理想信念并举。

　　本书是在课证融合的指导思想下,以职业能力提升为设计核心,基于教学过程将小学英语教学的典型工作任务细化,以专题和模块的形式将课程内容组织并有序展开的。全书共分为四个专题。第一专题是教学设计技能训练,包括教学设计概述、教学设计内容与方法,并提供了课时教学设计样例。第二专题是基本课型教学训练。以小学英语教学常见课型为训练模块,既有对课型教学的针对性介绍,又有具体教学策略和教学活动指导,使读者能够在短期内掌握小学英语教学核心技能。第三专题是基本技能训练,包括书写、简笔画和歌曲歌谣三项技能,技能知识讲授深入浅出,配合技能演示视频及真实教学案例。第四专题是教师资格证考试模拟训练,涵盖了面试和招考的三个主要内容,即面试、试讲和说课。本书的四个专题内容各有侧重,但编写思路一脉相承,并保持了递进性。简明的理论、真实的教学案例、详尽的案例分析贯穿全书。本书中的视频案例,读者可以通过扫描二维码观看,有助于直观形象地理解技能知识,提升教师职业技能训练效果。

　　本书可作为高校英语教育专业及小学教育专业课程的教材,也可以作为新入职小学英语教师的岗位培训教材;可供本科院校英语教育专业的学生选用,同时可作为广大教师资格证考试人员的备考用书。

　　最后,感谢本书责任编辑查莉女士为本书付出的辛勤劳动。由于作者水平有限,书中难免会存在不足与问题,恳请各位读者批评指正并提出宝贵意见。

目　录

专题四　教师资格证考试模拟训练

专题一

教学设计技能训练

◆ 了解教学设计的流程
◆ 掌握教学设计的基本方法
◆ 能够撰写具有完整教学流程的教学设计

师者,所以传道授业解惑也。作为一名合格的教师需要具备四种基本职业素养:教师职业道德素养、教师职业知识素养、教师职业能力素养和教师职业心理素养。教师资格证考试就是对这些素养的综合考查,其中"能力素养"方面的考查占有很大比重。为了让考生有针对性地准备教师资格证考试,高效地提升教师职业素养,本专题将从"教学设计"方面进行详述。

一、教学设计概述

教学设计是教师上好一节课的必要条件。美国学者肯普曾给教学设计下的定义是:"教学设计是运用系统方法分析研究教学过程中相互联系的各部分的问题和需求,在连续模式中确立解决它们的方法步骤,然后评价教学成果的系统计划过程。"在一线教学过程中,特别是在教师资格证面试过程中所提到的教学设计指的是"课时教学设计"。

课时教学设计是根据课程标准的要求和教学对象的情况,依照教育教学规律,运用一定的教学方法,对一课时的教学内容进行思考和设计。它一般包括教学背景分析、教学目标、教学重难点、教学资源、教学过程、板书设计等环节。为了达到良好的教学效果,在教学设计过程中需要关注以下几点:

◇ 准确性。在撰写教学设计之前,要对教学内容进行深入剖析,对教学内容中的语言知识、文化背景等要有准确的理解。执教者要充分研读资料后再进行备课,确保教学设计中的每一项内容正确,目标及重难点等项目准确。

◇ 全面性。教学设计是由一定的环节内容组成。在教学设计过程中,执教者要全盘构建,全面设计,不能缺项、漏项,保证教学设计的完整性。

◇ 科学性。教学设计的各个环节有一定的顺序,设计时要做到环环相扣,层层推进,先导入后新授,边新授边练习,有巩固,有拓展,有应用。这就要求教师在进行教学设计的过程中要考虑到各个环节之间的联系与关系,做到环节之间水到渠成,过渡语、衔接语自然不突兀。

◇ 情境性。小学英语强调趣味性,在解读文本时首先要考虑将文本内容放进一个什么样的情境中,让学生在具体的情境中感知、理解语言。

◇ 目标性。教学设计的形成是为了完成一定的教学目标。因此教学设计的每一个活动都要指向教学目标,确保每一项活动和任务的设置都为目标达成服务。

◇ 活动性。教学设计中的每一个环节指向一定的教学目标,每个环节又是由具体的活动组成的。所以教学设计时要突出活动性,用具体的活动去支撑教学内容的输入与输出。

✧ 层次性。教学设计中的活动不是随意设计的,它具有一定的层次性。单一活动往往是在综合活动之前,输入活动要在输出活动之前。此外,作业设置、板书设计也都要体现层次分明。

✧ 差异性。教学设计要尊重课型特点,不同课型要有自己的课型特色。例如:对话课要体现交际的功能,阅读课要体现对文本内容信息的分析、归纳、处理的功能等。

✧ 应用性。学以致用是教学的目的,通过学习发展综合语言应用能力,学生能够利用所学语言去解决实际生活中的问题。因此,在教学设计中要体现任务的实际应用功能,这就要求教师既要考虑适当的情境,又要考虑恰当的任务设置。

二、教学设计内容与方法

教学设计的撰写是在准确的背景分析之下,按照一定的流程进行的。具体来说,一次完整的教学设计按照如下流程进行:

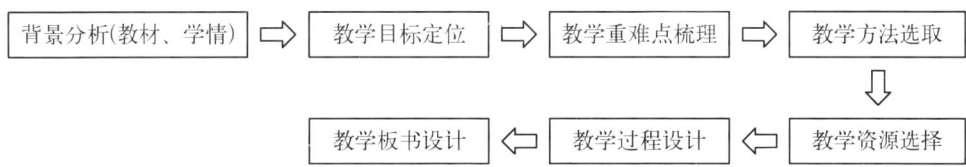

(一)教材分析

准确的教学内容分析是进行教学设计的前提。对一篇教学文本进行分析,要从三个方面着手:"基于课程标准的分析""基于学科核心素养的分析"和"基于文本内容的分析"。

1. 基于学科课程标准的分析

课程标准是撰写教学设计的依据。撰写教学设计之前必须清楚课程标准对本学科的要求,包括课程性质、课程理念、课程目标、课程内容、学业质量和课程实施等。

《义务教育英语课程标准(2022年版)》明确了以立德树人为根本任务的课程性质和课程理念,确立了围绕核心素养的课程目标,优化了课程内容、学业质量和课程实施。

课程性质:义务教育英语课程体现工具性和人文性的统一,具有基础性、实践性和综合性特征。学习和运用英语有助于学生形成跨文化沟通与交流的意识和能力,树立国际视野,涵养家国情怀,坚定文化自信,形成正确的三观,为学生终身学习、适应未来社会发展奠定基础。

课程理念:发挥核心素养的统领作用,构建基于分级体系的课程结构,以主题为引领,选择和组织课程内容,体现"学思结合、用创为本"的英语学习活动观,注重"教-学-评"一体化设计,推进信息技术与英语教学的深度融合。

2. 基于学科核心素养的分析

英语学科的核心素养包括语言能力、文化意识、思维品质和学习能力四个维度。语言能力就是运用语言解决问题的能力。在输入与输出过程中运用所学语言知识、语言意识和语感、语言技能、交际策略等进行听、说、读、看、写的能力。文化意识就是对中西方文化的认识

和理解，并在认知的过程中养成正确的人生观、价值观、世界观。在教学设计过程中，要关注教学内容中的中外文化，把知识内容放在全球化背景下，从知识素质、人文修养和行为取向等方面进行解读。思维品质，按照信息论的观点，思维是对新输入信息与脑内储存知识经验进行一系列复杂的心智操作过程。在小学英语教学中，思维品质可以理解为在对所学内容的学习过程中，学生反映出的分析、推理、判断、理性表达，同时能用英语进行多元思维等活动，并在活动中形成正确的思考辨析能力，提升其思维的逻辑性、批判性、创新性等。学习能力指在学习过程中学生能够运用一定的方式方法，有效地拓宽英语学习途径，提升英语学习效率的能力。

3. 基于文本内容的分析

文本解读是教师对教学内容（教材）进行认识、理解、分析和研究的过程，是准确定位教学目标和重难点、设计教学过程、撰写教学设计的前置行为。文本解读时，要"两看""两找""一理""一挖"。"两看"即看图片、看文字；"两找"找情境、找核心知识点。"一理"梳理主题意义；"一挖"挖掘文化价值。在文本解读过程中，要对教学设计进行情境化、问题化、活动化地分析，同时还要体现综合性、实践性和关联性的学习过程。

（二）学情分析

学情，从字面上简单理解就是学生的情况。学情分析就是对学生在教学过程中身心成长与发展相关的智力因素与非智力因素方面的研究和分析，是对教和学的过程与效果产生影响的学生学习信息的分析。换句话说，学情分析就是分析学生在学习过程中如何进行有效的学习，从而为教学设计和教学实践提供决策依据和策略指南。可以说，学情分析是教学整体设计的起点。

此外，学生作为学习的主体，在教与学的活动中，对教学内容的接收与掌握应是积极主动的，因而学情分析可以为"以学定教"提供理论依据。教师与学生的行为在课堂教学活动过程中都是实时的、动态的，教师应能够通过学生在活动中的注意力状态，回答问题的反应，课堂讨论的表现，课堂测试的效果等随时做出相应的教学调整，此时的学情分析可以为课堂教学提供教学实践的信息反馈。

根据学情分析的基本内涵，可以将其分为：教学前、教学过程中、教学后三个不同阶段的学情分析。

1. 教学前的学情分析

对于一名新入职的教师或教学经验尚不够丰富的年轻教师而言，教学前的学情分析是非常重要和必要的。俗话说，"知己知彼百战不殆"。教师走进课堂之前，如果能对自己即将面对的教学对象——学生做到"心中有数"，那么首先自己作为新教师的紧张情绪就会消除大半。教学前的学情分析主要包括：了解所教学生的知识背景，并根据教学内容的重难点，分析学生在学习过程中可能遇到的困难及其原因，以便针对性地加强指导。小学英语教学因不同地区、不同学区乃至不同的家庭背景而差异较大，比如有的小学生在上小学之前的幼儿阶段就已接触到较长时间的英语学习（如就读双语幼儿园），有的学校一年级开设英语课程，而有的学校三年级才开始开设英语课。小学生接触英语的初始时间各有不同，基础差距也较大，因此带来的学生对英语学习的兴趣、态度、习惯和方法也各有不同，这时的学情分析就需要着重对一个班集体的孩子进行详细了解，或根据英语基础进行分层次教学，或在教学过程中提出不同的教学要求，以使学有基础的学生保持兴趣，进一步提高；没有基础的学生激发兴趣，迅速进入学习状态，达到学习目标。

2. 教学中的学情分析

针对不同基础的学生，分析在学习过程中可能遇到的困难以及原因，予以不同的指导。在教学过程中，每个学生对同一教学内容的反应是各不相同的，但也有大致相同之处。比如，听讲的注意力是否集中，注意力能持续多久，对课堂活动是否积极参与，对课堂提问是否积极反应，这些共性的学情分析有助于教师在课堂教学实施过程中及时做出反馈；而学生的个性不同，如学习习惯、学习方法、学习的情绪与态度、具备的知识背景基础则是造成同一教学内容而教学效果各不相同的因素。

3. 教学后的学情分析

一堂课的教学结束，并不意味着教学活动的结束。教学后的学情分析既是对前一节课教学效果的反思，也为下一节教学计划的制定提供依据。教师不仅要在教案中对学生的学习过程进行反思，还要在作业批改中发现学生的学习态度是否端正、学习方法是否得当、学习目标是否达成。另外，通过课下个别交流或辅导、课外学习活动等方式，也可以了解学生在不同的学习环境下不同的学习状态与效果。

对于教学过程中各个环节的学情分析，不同的分析方法可以交互使用，以达到具体而最佳的效果。常用的方法包括理论分析法、资料分析法、经验分析法、整体观察法、个别访谈法、问卷调查法等。当下比较成熟的教育理论与学习理论，比如皮亚杰的认知发展阶段理论、建构主义理论、加德纳的多元智能理论等，可以为学情分析提供基本的分析依据、分析视角与分析方法。结合具体的学习对象、学习内容、学习环境以及学习过程等进行更加具体而深入的分析，揭示学习者的个性化学习特征，能够为教学活动提供更为具体和有针对性的指导信息。

（三）教学目标及重难点

1. 教学目标

教学目标是针对一定教学内容，通过教与学的过程之后期待学生达到的结果。教学目标的表述有三维目标、四维目标、五维目标等，虽然目标分类维度不同，但其包括的内容是大致相同的。针对不同的教学内容，可以选择不同的目标表达方式。以五维目标为例，教学目标分为语言技能目标、语言知识目标、情感态度目标、学习策略目标、文化意识目标。语言技能是语言运用能力的重要组成部分，主要包括听、说、读、看、写等方面的技能以及这些技能的综合运用。语言技能标准以学生"能做什么"为主要内容。例如："能够在真实或模拟的情境中运用句型……"；"能够运用核心词汇及句子完成……的任务"；"能够读出符合……发音规则的单词，并能够根据发音规则拼写出符合……发音规则的单词"等。语言知识是学生应该学习和掌握的英语语言知识。它包括语音、词汇、语法以及用于表达常见话题和功能的语言形式等。例如："能够认读句子……"；"读出字母……在单词中的发音是……"；"能够说出字母组合……的发音规则"等。情感态度指兴趣、动机、自信、意志和合作精神等影响学生学习过程和学习效果的相关因素，以及在学习过程中逐渐形成的祖国意识和国际视野。例如："学习对人有礼貌"；"能够合理安排日常学习和周末活动"等。学习策略指学生为了有效地学习和使用英语而采取的各种行动和步骤以及指导这些行动和步骤的信念。它包括认知策略、调控策略、交际策略和资源策略等。认知策略是指学生为了完成具体学习任务而采取的步骤和方法;调控策略是指学生对学习加以计划、实施、反思、评价和调整的行动和步骤;交际策略是学生为了争取更多的交际机会、维持交际以及提高交际效果而采取的行动;资源策略是学生合理并有效利用多种媒体进行学习和运用英语的方式和方法。例如:"学会与人沟通、交流个人信息";"能够在教师的帮助下总结名词性物主代词的规律,完成相应练习"等。文化意识是在教学过程中通过内容学习帮助学生了解所学语言国家的历史地理、风土人情、传统习俗、生活方式、行为规范、文学艺术、价值观念等。在学习英语的过程中,要帮助学生了解外国文化,提高对英语的理解和使用,增强对中华民族优秀传统文化的认识与热爱,加强全人类先进文化的熏陶,进一步培养国际意识。例如:"了解主要英语国家的国旗以及标志性建筑物"等。

例如:PEP《英语(三年级起点)》六年级上册 Unit 6 How do you feel? 中的 Let's talk。

教学目标:

① 能理解、朗读并背记核心词汇:feel, sad, angry, happy, worried, afraid。能感知、理解、正确朗读并书写核心句型 ... are afraid of ..., ... is angry with ...。

② 能在听前预测重点,能运用听力技巧完成听力任务。

③ 能在语境中感知、理解对话内容并能借助图文模仿读演对话,做到语言基本正确,表达比较流利并且有一定情感。

④ 能在语境中运用核心语言,对卡通片进行口头介绍,做到语音语调准确、内容完整达意、表达流利。

⑤ 识别卡通片中角色的感受;比较《黑猫警长》和《猫和老鼠》猫鼠角色异同。

2. 教学重难点

教学重点与教学难点是在教学目标正确定位和学情准确分析的基础上梳理出来的。教学重点一般是学生必须掌握的知识与技能。如,根据课标要求学生必须要掌握理解的核心句子与核心词汇等。教学难点是指学生不易理解的知识或不易掌握的技能技巧。难点不一定是重点,也有些内容既是难点又是重点。

例如:《英语(三年级起点)》六年级上册 Unit 6 How do you feel?中的 Let's talk 课时内容的教学重难点。

教学重点:能在语境中借助图文模仿读演对话。

教学难点:chases 的发音;能在语境中运用核心语言,对卡通片进行口头介绍。

(四)教学方法

教学方法是指教师为了完成教学任务所使用的工作手段或方法。现代英语教学法流派多种多样,既有从国外外语教学中形成并流传到我国而广泛沿用的教学方法,也有适应中国英语教育新形势发展而越来越多引起关注和进行实践的新方法。不同时期的外语教学在不同的社会背景下其教学理念也不尽相同。我国外语教学法在开始阶段基本上是学习借鉴西方的教学法,其中对我国外语教学产生深刻影响的传统教学法主要有:全身反应法、交际法、直接法、听说法、视听法、翻译法等。

1. 全身反应法(Total Physical Response,简称TPR)

该教学法产生于20世纪六七十年代的美国,创始人是心理学教师阿舍儿(James T. Asher)。这种教学法是根据指令做动作,通过理解指令,再进一步衍生出更多相关动作,从而使学生在行动中熟悉并掌握词语和句型。老师作为TPR的指导者,给学生提供练习的机会,达到寓教于乐的目的。

2. 交际法(Communicative Approach)

交际法也叫功能法或意念法,形成于20世纪六七十年代。它提出交际既是学习的目的也是学习手段,强调教学要为交际需要服务,主张模拟各种语境,为学生提供综合运用英语语言进行交际的机会。交际法注重的不仅是语言的准确性,更强调语言使用的得体性。

3. 直接法(Direct Method)

直接法是在19世纪下半叶随着国际间交流日益增强语言作为交际的功能凸显而产生的。德国外语教育家菲埃托最早提出这一教学法。它针对翻译法不能培养学生听说能力的缺点,主张以口语材料为教学内容,直接学习,直接理解,直接应用。它强调模仿,用教儿童学习本族语言的方法来学习外语。直接法在培养口语能力方面取得了显著成绩,但对母语在外语学习中的作用认识不足,对母语与外语学习的规律差别不够重视。

4. 听说法(Audio-lingual Method)

听说法源自二战期间的美国,其理论基础是美国结构主义语言学和行为主义心理学。它强调在外语学习过程中,听说领先,反复操练,以句型为中心,运用各种现代化视听手段进行教学。缺点是对读写重视不够,句型操练脱离语境,不利于培养创造性地运用语言的交际能力。

5. 视听法(Audio-Visual Method)

视听法吸取了直接法和听说的许多优点,充分利用各种现代化视听工具和手段,使学生边看边听边说,身临其境地学习外语。这种方法重视口语教学和句型教学,强调情境与语言相结合,更符合学生交际的需要。但是此法忽视语言分析、讲解和训练,不利于理解外语能力的培养。

6. 翻译法 (Translation Method)

翻译法作为一种教学方法历史可追溯到欧洲中世纪,曾对我国的外语教学产生深远的影响。其突出的特点是用语法讲解加翻译练习的方式来教外语。由于此法重视语法教学又被称为语法法或语法翻译法。此方法有利于学生集中掌握语法规则,有利于培养学生理解外语和运用外语的能力。但是翻译法只重视书面语,忽略了语言交际能力的培养,而且此法教学方式单一,课堂气氛沉闷,不易引起学习兴趣。

除了前面所提到的外语教学法之外,还有一些教学方式方法虽影响不那么广泛,但在某些学习阶段也有比较明显的效果,尤其针对小学阶段的英语教学值得思考与借鉴。

7. 任务型教学 (Task-based Language Teaching)

任务型教学兴起于20世纪80年代,是教师通过引导学生在课堂上完成任务来进行教学。它强调的是"做中学",这种教学方法是交际教学法的发展,在我国的基础英语课堂教学改革中逐渐形成主流。在教学活动中教师根据特定的交际和语言项目设计出具体可操作的任务,学生通过各种语言交际活动参与完成任务,以达到学习和掌握语言的目的。

8. 歌曲歌谣教学 (Teaching English through Songs, Rhymes and Chants)

歌曲歌谣富于童趣、易学易唱、深受少儿的喜爱。它语言地道,歌词简短,不断重复,便于记忆,符合语言学习规律。英语语音语调的训练及朗读能力的提高离不开音高、音长、重音、节奏、速度、连读、失去爆破等知识和技能。学唱英语歌曲和歌谣不但能自然而然地学习这些知识和技能,还能够创设轻松的学习氛围,培养学习英语的兴趣,陶冶情操。利用歌曲歌谣进行英语教学是促进语言能力发展的有效途径。

9. 多模态教学 (Multi-modal Teaching)

多模态教学主张调动学生的多种感官协同运作,学生通过多种身体力行的体验提高学习兴趣,以达到加深印象强化记忆的目的。它倡导语言教学与其他非语言教学相结合,利用多种渠道多种教学手段通过不同的媒介把静态资源和动态资源纳入教学过程共同参与教学。

小学英语教学方法丰富多样,每一种教学方法都各有优缺点,各种教学方法也不是一成不变的。俗话说"教学有法,教无定法,贵在得法",要设计和实施有效的教学活动,首先要明确"以学生为中心"的教学思想,最大限度地发挥学生的主观能动性;其次要结合学生的基础和课堂教学目标并根据授课类型和学习内容,充分利用现代化设施条件,有机整合各种教学方法,让学生在英语学习中既掌握语言知识,又掌握语言技能,从而发展英语语言综合运用能力。

(五) 教学过程

教学过程包含导入、新授、练习、巩固、拓展、作业等环节。

1. 导入

导入环节是一节课的起始环节,一个好的导入将有助于提升整节课的效果,正所谓"好的导入是成功课例的一半"。导入环节设计要简洁,抓住学生心理,通过有趣的形式,让学生思维以最快的速度投入课堂中,进而调动学生的注意力,激发学生的学习兴趣,形成"虎头"之势。在此环节,一般采用情景对话导入、故事导入、歌曲导入、猜谜导入、chant

导入、视频导入、图片导入等。同时,在导入环节要精选内容,使其与新授内容高度相关,进而让导入环节为新授内容的学习做好铺垫。此环节教师要把控好时间,一般控制在2—4分钟左右。

2. 新授

新授环节是教学过程的主要部分。在此环节中教师要根据课型特点设计有效的教学活动,帮助学生学习新知识和练习新知识。词汇课中的新授要注意"词不离句",即在句子中学习词汇、练习词汇和应用词汇。对话课中要突出"交际"功能,在话轮中进行有效学习。阅读课中要重视对文章意义的整体把握和阅读方法的指导。语音课中关注把发音规律规则的知识内容放进任务活动的探究中,让学生在对某一规律的自我探究、合作和总结的过程中进行学习和应用。

3. 练习

练习环节是针对新授内容,通过不同形式的任务活动进行记忆、内化。此环节通常被设计为三个不同难度的进阶式活动:机械性练习(mechanical drills)、有意义的练习(meaningful drills)和交际性练习(communicative drills)。机械性练习是对所学语言知识进行反复的重复练习或替换练习。在有意义的练习中,教师仍然控制学生的答案,学生对新语言的操练被限制在一定的框架中。交际性练习是语言输出练习的高阶活动,旨在培养学生在真实语境中运用所学的能力。练习活动的设计要遵循先重复后模仿再应用的原则。此处的练习,由于后跟巩固、拓展等环节,确切地说是通过反复的练习来学习的一种方式,即机械性练习。

4. 巩固

巩固环节是练习环节的延伸,帮助学生整体掌握和内化"课时内容"。在练习与巩固环节中,练习环节突出活动的"单一性",即针对某一个知识点的小练习;而巩固环节更突出活动的"综合性",起到全面应用新知识的作用。新授、练习、巩固三个环节,环环相扣,层层递进。教师设计活动要丰富多样,做到有学有练。学生在边学边练中逐步巩固所学。

5. 拓展

拓展环节是一节课的高潮部分,是检验一节课学习目标是否达成的重要环节,也是课时内容教育升华的重要步骤。在拓展环节中,教师要带着所学知识走进学生的"学习生活"和"社会生活"。教师要根据教学内容恰当地选择、创设、模拟学习生活和社会生活场景,设计相对应的任务,让学生用所学的知识去解决实际问题,做到学以致用,真正发挥语言的工具性功能。同时,教师在教学设计时还要在内容和活动的推进中提炼出正确的思想引导、价值判断,进而落实情感态度教育,提升德育教育。德育内容的呈现不能生拉硬套,让学生感到突兀。要多让学生参与,给学生留有思考时间,通过小组合作等形式使德育润物无声、水到渠成,形成"画龙点睛"之笔,最终让拓展环节形成一节课的"龙尾"之势。

6. 作业

作业环节是一节课的课后延伸,作业的设计要体现基础性、拓展性和层次性。一般情况下可以设计"必选作业"突出基础巩固练习,"选修作业"突出能力的拓展。进而形成作业超市,让每一位学生都能够根据自己的水平和特点选择。

7. 教学过程设计样例

PEP《英语（三年级起点）》六年级（上册）
Unit 6 How do you feel? 中的 Let's talk 教学过程设计

Teaching steps	Teachers' activities
I. Warm-up	Look and say. Guide the students to review the words and sentences about 5 feelings. Such as: happy, sad, angry, worried and afraid.

II. Presentation	Let's talk.
	1. T: Do you like cartoons? Sarah and Sam are going to watch a cartoon.
	  Guide them to think about a question: What's this cartoon about? → Watch the video and find out the answer. → It's about a cat.
	  T: What does he do? → The cat is a police officer.
	  Ask the students to read it one by one. → mouse mice
	2. Ask the students to watch the video again and try to find out: The cat is _____. The mice are _____ of him.
	  → The cat is angry.
	  → The mice are afraid of him.
	  → WHY is the cat angry with the mice? → Because the mice are bad. They hurt people.

III. Practice	1. Listen and imitate. 2. Shadow reading. Ask them to read with the video. 3. Read and act in roles. Practice the dialogue in pairs, and then show it. 4. Let's sing. *Cat, cat. Cool, cool, cool!* *He chases the mice.* *Mice, mice. Bad, bad, bad.* *They're afraid of him.* *The mice are bad.* *The mice are bad.* *The cat is angry with them.* *The mice are bad.* *The mice are bad.* *La la la la la la la.* *The mice are bad.*
IV. Production	1. Ask the students to introduce the cartoon *Mr. Black*. 2. Ask the students to introduce another cartoon about cat and mouse: *Tom and Jerry*. 3. Ask the students to talk about their favorite cartoons.
V. Homework	Get more information about your favorite cartoon and try to introduce it in English.

(六)板书设计

板书是一节课主要内容或者核心语言的板面呈现。有效的板书设计有助于学生加深理解课时内容。板书设计要突出"中心",形成主次之分,帮助学生有效记忆主板书的核心内容。同时,板书设计要突出"美",根据内容可设计趣味性强的"图案",激发学生学习兴趣。

◇ 板书设计样例一:

优点:1. 板面美观。

　　　2. 板书内容有效地突出了教学文本的核心内容。

　　　3. 设计突出了文本背后的教育功能。"饮食金字塔"让学生直观地感知到"健康饮食"的具体内容。

存在问题:

　　　1. 教师书写水平有待提高。

　　　2. 板书设计中,对话书写呈现的位置不凸显,不能有效地突出它的重要性。

◇ 板书设计样例二:

优点:1. 图案与教学内容相关度大,能让学生形象直观地感知教学内容。

　　　2. 结构图使用合理,房子结构图案在无形中渗透家庭观念。

存在问题:

　　　1. 教师书写水平有待提高。

　　　2. 缺少家庭友爱的渗透,可在图案中加入一颗爱心,表达家是有爱的地方。

◇ 板书设计样例三:

优点:1. 图形与教学主题相关。表的中心是核心问句,与周边的核心词汇形成对话。

　　　2. 设计上体现时间规划意图,具有一定的思维培养功能。

存在问题:

　　　1. 文字内容书写不规范,颜色使用不合理。

　　　2. 图案内容不精准。

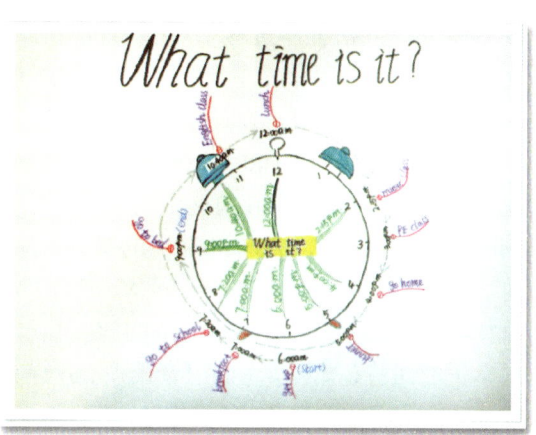

❖ 板书设计样例四：

优点：1. 板书内容体现了文化意识和国际视野。

2. 思维导图运用巧妙，有助于学生清晰地构建学习框架和发散思维的培养。

存在问题：

1. 教师书写质量有待提高。

2. 课题板书缺少。

3. 内容布局欠妥。如，加拿大位置可以放到板面右上区域。

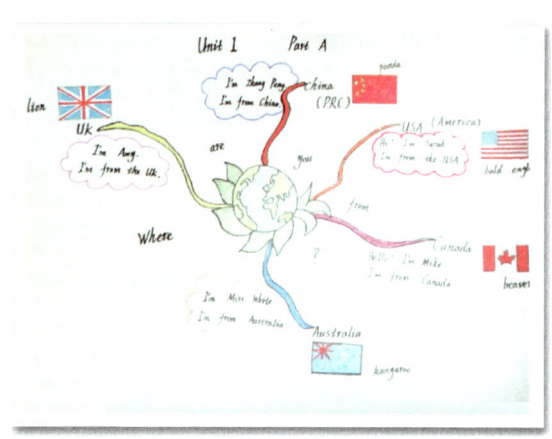

（七）教学评价

教学评价是依据教学目标对教学过程及结果进行价值判断并为教学决策服务的活动，是对教学活动现实的或潜在的价值做出判断的过程。著名课程专家崔允漷教授曾经指出：评价不只是考试和测验，评价还是对学习做出估量，更重要的是促使学习变得更有意义和价值；评价也不只是笔试或告知分数，更重要的是采用与目标匹配的多样方法，对学习过程和结果进行基于学情的处理、解释与反馈。作为一名教师，必须具备必要的评价素养，灵活使用各种评价手段，将评价镶嵌在教学中，教学与评价融为一体，发挥评价作为教学定位系统的作用，让教师随时了解学生的位置和将要去的方向。

教学评价一般包括形成性评价（formative assessment）和终结性评价（summative assessment）。课程应注重评价形式的多样化，将形成性评价和终结性评价结合使用，既关注学习的结果，又关注学习的过程。基础教育阶段的英语学习强调以形成性评价为主。形成性评价是对学生学习过程中的表现，所取得的成绩以及所反映出的情感、态度、策略方面的发展做出评价。例如学习了有关教室和文具的课文后，不只是测试学生从中学到的语法和词汇知识，还要学生学会物品的摆放整理，知道在教室、家庭、公共场合不能做的事情等；从有关旅行的课文中学到如何规划行程，综合考虑天气、交通、食宿等因素后，与同行者沟通做出最佳选择。从这些例子可以看出，形成性评价可以引导学生思考，分析问题和解决问题，让他们运用批判性思维的技能，进行比较、归纳、反思，对学生的深度学习具有极大的促进作用。

评价既包括教学过程中对教师的评价，也包括学校或者教师对学生学习效果的评价，这里我们提到的评价，主要指对学生学习效果的评价。以下面的 What's in my schoolbag? 一课为例，看一看评价在课堂教学中的作用。首先，教师问 What's in your schoolbag? Then look at my schoolbag and guess what's in it? (Pay attention to the rising and falling tones) 用游戏引发学生兴趣，学生在猜谜语的同时，使用了已有的语言知识。教师继续问：What do you think of my schoolbag? 通过学生的描述，教师知道学生已有的关于书包的认知水平，教师向学生介绍 Wimpy Kid Grey，问 What's in his schoolbag? What's in your schoolbag, Grey? 教师在与学生的互动中，介绍本课的学习目标。接着问学生 What's in your schoolbag? 教师通过学生的回答，检测学生的语音语调，进行有针对性的练习。抛出问题 What do you want to say to Grey? 引导学生使用语言，这其实既是教学，又是评价，学生回答 A. Oh, your schoolbag is a mess. B. Oh, your schoolbag is untidy. C... 学生讨论自己的书包，教师让学生汇报讨论的结果，对学生的汇报进行评价。接下来让学生用句子来进行写作训练 I have three _____, an _____, a _____ and _____ in my schoolbag. 然后同桌之间用这个句式互动提问，教师做出评价。教师提问学生：What's in your desk? 学生会使用刚才的句型进行回答。教师再次提出更高的要求：不仅回答 I have ... in my desk. 还要说出 My schoolbag/desk/...is _____。

再以 PEP 四下 Unit 3 Weather 中的 Part B Let's talk 一课为例，看一看评价在课堂教学中的作用。首先，在热身阶段呈现冷热暖凉四种温度的图片，教师问 Is it cold/hot/warm/cool? 教师继续引导学生关注 Mark 的图片，提醒学生观察其衣着（T恤）并问 Is it cold? 学生结合生活体验和已有知识进行判断。教师在与学生的互动中，渗透了本课学习目标之一的一般疑问句 Is it cold? 及其答语。接下来引导学生关注 Mark 与 Chen Jie 的对话话题。然后教师进一步提问 How do they talk about weather in New York/Beijing? 引导学生发现目标语言，使用目标语言。这既是教学，又是不断评价的过程。学生能够回答 What's the weather like in New York? How about Beijing? Is it cold? 然后让学生运用这些语句谈论天气，并让学生到讲台上进行天气播报，这是对学生能否流利使用目标语的评价。然后进行 Listen and imitate，学生跟读过程中教师注意学生是否能够准确发音，语调是否自然，这是教师就学生使用语言的准确性进行的评价。接下来在拓展阶段，在教师的帮助下学生能够进入有特定情境的对话，如向自己在外地的亲人打电话，通过电话询问天气，表达关心的情感。学生不仅要使用目标语，还要进行一定程度的创编，能完成 3—4 个话轮的交流，这是教师对学生使用语言的准确性、流利性和复杂性进行评价。

三、课时教学设计样例

PEP《英语（三年级起点）》四年级上册 Unit 4 My Home 中的 Let's learn
【设 计 者】枣庄市实验小学　褚洪静

（一）教材内容

本课是 PEP《英语（三年级起点）》四年级上册 Unit 4　My Home 单元 B 部分的第四课时，具体的教学内容包括 Let's learn 和 Let's do 两部分，其中 Let's learn 部分的主要词汇有：phone、fridge、TV、sofa、table、shelf、bed；Let's do 部 分要求学生听懂六个短语：Sit on the sofa/Make the bed/Watch TV/Answer the phone/Open the door/Set the table，学习话题与学生的生活有着紧密的联系。教师的主要教学设计应该遵循单词教学词不离句

的原则，抓住单词在生活中的运用形态，在单词的趣味练习和拓展练习上做文章。

（二）学生分析

本课的学习主体是四年级学生。他们从三年级就开始了系统的英语学习，对英语表现出

强烈的好奇心和兴趣,已经建立了英语学习的意识,储备了一定的英语词汇,具备了简单的英语语言运用能力,他们在课堂上表现出积极参与课堂和乐于表达的优秀品质。对于本课内容来说,学习的场景就是学生熟悉的环境,学生每天生活在这个环境里,所以他们会更加乐于参与本课的学习活动。但考虑到学生特点,fridge, table和shelf单词的发音应该是个难关。

(三)教学目标

1. 知识目标

① 能听、说、认读phone, fridge, TV, sofa, table, shelf, bed等词汇。

② 能听懂本课Let's do部分的指令语并根据指令做出相应的动作,如:Sit on the sofa/Make the bed/Watch TV/Answer the phone/Open the door/Set the table。

2. 技能目标

能在相关语境中熟练运用本课词汇phone, fridge, TV, sofa, table, shelf, bed和节奏中的指令语。

3. 情感态度与学习策略

① 学生能了解中西方餐具摆放礼仪的差异并能正确地摆放西方的餐具。

② 学生能了解常见辅音的发音规则,形成一定的认读策略。

③ 学生通过帮助老师设计新家活动,锻炼空间思维能力和设计能力;通过了解一些常见的家居用品品牌,提高生活实践能力。

④ 学生能体会家不在于大小、不在于家具的多少,家是蕴含着亲情的地方。

(四)教学重难点

① 重点:听懂、会说、认读本课的家具和生活用品词,在相关情境中运用指令语Sit on the sofa/Make the bed/Watch TV/Answer the phone/Open the door/Set the table。

② 难点:fridge, shelf, table单词的发音;听指令,做动作。

(五)教学准备

PPT、一套西式餐具(包括刀、叉、盘子等),一套中式餐具(包括筷子、勺子和碗等),教师准备几把办公的椅子当作沙发供做游戏用,教师打印房间平面结构图,发给每小组一张,教师准备各种家具的小贴画若干,每个学习小组准备一套橡皮泥。

(六)教学过程

Step 1. Warm up

教师在黑板上板书一个房子框架作为板书的样式,为后来往相应的房间里板书单词和简笔画做铺垫。

【设计意图】通过板书房屋框架,既可以营造直观、有效的情境,使板书美观、明了,又能够给学生留下深刻的印象,激发学习动机。

（1）自由会话,激活旧知。

T: Children, I have a new house in front of our school. It's in Ziguangyuan（作者小区名称）.

PPT呈现教师小区房子外景图,创设情境,带学生参观教师的房子,然后呈现其内部房屋结构的图纸,让学生了解教师的房屋结构,并通过下面的填空题考查学生对本单元A部分房间名称的掌握情况。

T: What's it like? Now, come and visit my new house and fill in the blanks.

There are _____ bedrooms, _____ bathrooms, _____, _____ and _____. Wow, it's so big!

【设计意图】带学生参观教师的房子能够激发学生的好奇心,保证了语言实践的情境性和真实性,同时复习了A部分的房间名称,一举多得。

（2）快乐节奏,再次操练。

教师把全班分成两组,一组学生说去哪个房间,另外一组迅速地反应,并做出相应的动作,教师表扬反应快的学生和动作到位的学生。

T: Now, let's chant in groups.

eg: Group 1: Go to the living room.　　　　Group 2: Watch TV. Act it out.
　　　Group 1: Go to the kitchen.　　　　　Group 2: Have a snack. Act it out.

【设计意图】教师创新了节奏的使用方法,分组让学生进行节奏的说唱比赛和表演比赛,既可以在最短时间内有效地集中学生的注意力,又可以让练习层次从机械操练的层面提升到意义操练的层面。从Free talk到Let's chant的环节过渡水到渠成,浑然一体。

Step 2. Presentation

（1）情境引路,顺利导入。

教师出示教师的空房子,创设即将装修房子的情境,让学生为教师提出购置家居生活用品的建议。

T: Children, look at my new house. It's empty now. What shall I buy for my new house? Can you make a plan for me?

S1: A TV. S2: A bed. S3: 冰箱。S4: 餐桌和椅子。S5: 沙发。S6: 书橱,电视柜。

T: Thank you for your advice. Let's learn them one by one.

【设计意图】教师创设即将装修房子的情境,利用小学生乐于助人的特点让他们为老师购置家居用品提出建议,一方面可以激发学生的学习动机,另一方面又可以自然过渡到新知的呈现。

（2）游戏贯穿,学有所练。

教师通过PPT呈现学生建议老师购置的家居用品,逐一学习本课新单词。（根据学生的随机回答调整单词教学的顺序）

① 有奖竞猜,现学现卖。

教学单词：bed。

在黑板上房子框架内的一间卧室里画一张床的简笔画,在简笔画上板书bed一词并用红色的粉笔标出b,d两个辅音字母。教师教读单词,让学生注意单词中的辅音字母并让学

生拼读单词中的字母,通过简单的节奏让学生记住这一单词。

B, b, b, /b/　/b/　/b/

E, e, e, /e/　/e/　/e/

D, d, d, /d/　/d/　/d/

/b/　/e/　/d/　bed, it's a bed.

教师设计猜的游戏,让学生猜测老师需要购置几张床。

T: How many beds do I need? Guess, please.

S1: A bed. S2: Two beds. S3: Three beds. T: Yes, you're right.

教师出示家庭成员照片,公布猜测结果,并奖励床的小贴画。

T: I need a bed for me and two beds for my son and my parents.

【设计意图】教师通过简笔画,给学生提供简单、直观的语境,让学生迅速建立单词的音、义和形之间的联系。通过语音教学,可以帮助学生突破认读关,逐步掌握常见发音规则。教师设计的猜测游戏,既可以让学生有意义地练习新词汇,又可以培养学生的思维能力。

② 抢沙发游戏,"抢"到学生们的兴趣。

教学单词: sofa。

在黑板上房子框架内的客厅里画一张沙发的简笔画,在简笔画上面板书sofa一词,并用红色的粉笔标出s, f两个辅音字母。教师教读单词,让学生注意单词中的辅音字母并让学生拼读单词,通过简单的节奏让学生准确记住它的语音。

S, s, s, /s/　/s/　/s/　f, f, f, /f/　/f/　/f/.

sofa, sofa, sofa, it's a sofa.

抢沙发游戏:

PPT出示扶手椅和沙发两幅图,让学生了解它们的不同。告诉学生沙发是个外来词,要注意元音字母o 和a的发音。

教师准备四把椅子充当沙发,把"沙发"围成一圈,找五个学生到前面来围成一圈,教师说明游戏规则:游戏开始时,前面的五个学生围着沙发慢跑,并注意听教师指令,大家拍手齐说: Sofa, sofa, it's a sofa. 当老师说: Sit on the sofa. 大家开始抢沙发,抢不到的淘汰出局。继续玩游戏3次,并奖励沙发贴画给参与游戏的学生。

【设计意图】利用抢沙发游戏趣味操练单词sofa,不仅可以活跃学习气氛,还能够加深学生对sofa这一单词的意义理解。

③ 餐具摆一摆,摆出中西方文化各自的精彩。

教学单词: table。

在黑板上房子框架内的餐厅里画一张餐桌的简笔画,在简笔画上面板书table一词,并用红色的粉笔标出t, b, l三个辅音字母。教师教读单词,找学生领读单词,让学生注意单词中的辅音字母并让学生拼读单词,通过简单的节奏让学生准确识记语音。

摆餐桌游戏:

教师将一张桌布盖在讲桌上,并拿出事先准备好的筷子、刀、叉、碗和碟。教师说明选人办法:谁能把I can set the table.说好,谁就可以到前面来摆餐具。练习好I can set the table.后,找几个学生到前面来摆餐具,边摆边说: I can set the table.先摆中式的餐具,再摆放西式的餐具。教师给予正确的指导。

【设计意图】通过摆餐桌游戏，既可以让学生直观地建立语音和动作的联系，又可以让学生在动手实践中了解中西方餐具礼仪的文化差异。

④ 我的书橱你帮选，滚动练习来一遍。

用上面教单词的办法教学shelf一词。

PPT呈现不同颜色、不同风格（中式和欧式）的书橱，让学生帮老师推荐书橱并给出建议。如：The white shelf is the most beautiful.

T: Can you tell me which shelf is the most beautiful one? You may say: The yellow/blue/white... shelf is the most beautiful one.

S1: The blue shelf is the most beautiful one.

S2: The orange shelf is the most beautiful one.

S3: ...

T: Let me think it over. I will choose the white shelf. White shelf is a good match for my room. You're so kind. Thank you.

【设计意图】推荐书橱活动既可以突破shelf的语音关，又可以让学生在情境中实践运用这一词汇，同时能激发学生的语言运用热情。

⑤ 电话礼仪知多少，课堂、生活链接好。

PPT出示电话的图片，用上面教单词的办法教学phone一词。运用集体读和个体读相结合的方式，边读边让学生做接电话的动作：Answer the phone.

PPT出示接打电话的礼貌用语和不恰当用语让学生选择。

T: There are some sentences about phoning. Choose the right one.

S1: ...

S2: ...

【设计意图】TPR活动的使用旨在让学生有效建立音形义的联系，同时渗透礼仪教育。

⑥ 我选冰箱你帮忙，情感目标不要忘。

用上面教单词的办法教学fridge一词。

教师继续铺设需要购买冰箱的语言环境，PPT出示各种品牌的冰箱（冰箱上有放大的品牌名称），让学生给老师提出购买建议。

T: Oh, children. Let me think, I need a fridge.

T: Which one should I choose?

S1: Songxia fridge.

T: Panasonic fridge.

S2: Haier fridge.

S3: ...

T: Thank you for your advice. I will choose Haier fridge.

【设计意图】选冰箱活动旨在让学生突破语音关，同时渗透支持国产品牌的情感教育。

（3）教师播放本课单词部分录音，学生跟读，让学生画出单词里面的辅音字母，并注意它们的发音。

eg: ph, sh, f, r, t, b, s, f, b, d

【设计意图】让学生标注单词里的辅音,帮助他们逐步掌握辅音的发音规则,可以降低学生的认读难度,有助于逐步解决认读难这一问题。

Step 3. Practise

(1)小组练习:四人一小组,一人出示单词的图片,其他三人快速地说出单词。然后,其他人依次轮流出示图片。

(2) PPT出示填空连线题。

让学生独立完成此题,然后核对答案。

It's a _e_.

It's a _ridge.

It's a _ _ one.

It's a she_ _.

It's a _o_a.

It's a ta_le.

(3)搬家游戏。

PPT出示一个带有各种家具的房子,让学生在短时间内记住房子里有哪些家具,然后出示下一张幻灯片,让学生迅速找出哪一样家具被搬走了。

T: What's missing?

S1: A phone. S2: A shelf. S3: ...

【设计意图】通过以上三个活动由易到难,层次递进,夯实本课的操练效果,同时可以让学生建立本课词汇音义形之间的联系。

（4）学生听音乐完成Let's chant。教师先让学生看图说句子,然后再跟随音乐做动作。

T: At home, we should do some housework. Let's see what Sarah and Wu Binbin do at home.

eg: Answer the phone/set the table/Make the bed.

（5）TPR活动。

教师带领学生做TPR活动,让学生用动作表示出相关短语。

T: Now, children. Let's play a game. I say the words. You try to do the right actions.

T: shelf   Ss: Read a book. Do the action.

S1: fridge   Ss: Open the fridge. Do the action.

S2: table   Ss: Set the table. Do the action.

【设计意图】chant和TPR两个做动作的递进式活动,既能够起到趣味操练活跃气氛的目的,又有利于实现本课的语用功能。

Step 4. Production

PPT出示教师房间平面结构图,教师继续拓展情境,学生小组合作帮助教师选择家具并摆放入相应的房间,设计出合理的摆放位置。

T: Now, children, can you help me to design my new house? Choose furniture and put them into the right places. Try to be a good designer. Come on!

让小组展示设计出来的家居用品摆放效果,并做简单介绍。教师点评,引出家人间的和谐相处对于一个家来说才是最重要的。

Group 1: This is a living room. There is a TV and a red sofa. This is a kitchen. There is a Haier fridge and a table...

Group 2: This is a study. There is a blue shelf, a desk and a chair.

T: As for a family, which do you think is the most important thing?

S1: ...

S2: ...

T: The families live happily. Everyone in the family loves each other and helps each other. That is the most important thing.

【设计意图】通过为老师设计新家的活动,锻炼学生的设计能力;学生展示活动让学生认识到家不在大小和家具的多少,而在于家人之间的和谐相处。

Step 5. Summary

梳理所学内容,使学生对本课内容形成一个整体认识。

Step 6. Homework

（1）学生在家里跟读录音,准确模仿。

（2）用橡皮泥捏家具并说一说。

（3）画出自己理想中的家并在下一节课展示。

【设计意图】教师设计了3项作业,第一项是必做作业,第二、三项作业为选做作业。学生根据自己的爱好特长等自由选择。这样既可以照顾学生的差异,又可以培养学生深层的学习兴趣,让学生在玩中做到复现、巩固语言。

Step 7. Blackboard design

四、课后训练

请根据PEP《英语（三年级起点）》三年级上册Unit 2 Colours中的Let's talk设计一份课时教学设计。

专题二

基本课型教学训练

一、词汇教学概述

词汇是语言学习的基础。著名语言学家D. A. Wilkins曾经说过Very little can be communicated if there is no grammar; nothing can be communicated if there is no vocabulary。词汇在语言交际中占有举足轻重的地位。词汇教学是小学英语教学的重要组成部分。

词汇指语言中所有单词和固定短语的总和。词汇中的任何词语都是通过一定的句法关系和语义关系与其他词语建立起联系的,并在语境中传递信息。目前被广泛使用的不同版本的小学英语教材就是基于这一理念编写的。如PEP《英语(三年级起点)》(人民教育出版社)中的Let's learn部分,《英语(牛津上海版)》(上海教育出版社)中的Look and learn部分,都是专门针对词汇进行学习的板块。以PEP《英语(三年级起点)》(人民教育出版社)四年级上册中的Unit 3 Let's learn部分为例,它是将对词汇"tall and strong, short and thin, friendly, quiet"的教学与句式结构"I have a good friend. He's..."结合,将对描写人的形容词学习置于介绍人的真实生活语境中。

有的教材并没有将词汇学习这一板块单独设立,而是将词汇的教学放置在一定的情境中,以对话或者故事文本为载体教授词汇,帮助学生正确使用词汇

开展有意义的语言交流,侧重语言运用功能。

教授词汇要关注词汇的"音、形、义、用"四个方面。词音学习是词汇学习的基础。教授词汇时要确保词音正确,可以通过播放音视频等多种手段输入,让学生感知词音,再通过模仿朗读等各种语音练习达到词音输出准确无误。词形的学习主要是指词的拼写。引导学生将单词拼写与读音规则结合起来,运用拼读规则按照音节读单词,进行学法指导,逐步培养学生按发音规则拼读和记忆单词的习惯和能力。词汇只有在理解词义的基础上才可以运用。教授词义时,注意不要把英语单词和汉语的词在意思上完全等同起来,尽量不要使用翻译法,多利用实物、图画、动作和手势等直观的方法来建立词音、词形与词义的联系,帮助学生理解词义。对词汇"音形义"的掌握不是词汇教学的终点,能够"运用"才是终极目标。无论是在学习和巩固词汇的"音形义"时,还是在练习"使用"词汇时,都要结合一定的语言情境。最终落实在真实语境中运用语言,即将所学语言用于解决实际问题。

二、常用教学方法与活动

1. 呈现、练习词汇的方法

（1）直观呈现。

采用实物、图片、简笔画、多媒体等辅助教具或者表情、动作等呈现新词,是小学英语词汇教学常用的方法。小学生形象思维能力较强,抽象思维能力较弱,更易于接受感性的、形象的、具体的事物。提供可视的媒介或者用身体演示词汇意义的方法符合小学生的认知特点。小学英语大部分词汇也适合使用形象直观的呈现方式展示。

以PEP《英语（三年级起点）》三年级上册Unit 5 Let's eat为例,在学习词汇"milk, bread, egg, juice"时教师可以使用实物呈现的方式教授。结合实物形象生动、表意直观的特点,不但能帮助学生迅速、准确了解词义,而且能培养学生观察力、想象力,激发学习兴趣。

小学英语词汇中的动词多为具体的行为动词,适合以形象的动作呈现。在教授PEP《英语（三年级起点）》五年级上册Unit 4 What can you do?中的新词汇"swim, play basketball, play ping-pong"时,教师可以通过边做动作边说单词的方式让学生建立词义和词音的联系,使学生更直观地体悟词汇的意义。

（2）创设情境。

义务教育阶段的英语课程提倡采用既

强调语言学习过程,又有利于提高学生学习成效的语言教学途径和方法,尽可能多地为学生创造在真实语境中运用语言的机会。教授词汇时利用语境,学生在学习词的音形义的同时根据上下文推测词义,还能明确词汇所运用的具体语言情境。这种方法能帮助学生发展学习策略,培养语言学习能力和逻辑推理能力,进而逐渐形成自主学习意识。

PEP《英语(三年级起点)》五年级上册Unit 3 What would you like?就可以通过创设去快餐店点餐这一语境学习"ice cream, hamburger, salad"等词汇。快餐食品的名称及表达自己对食物的喜好,这些内容是在日常生活中经常用到的,是真实生活经验的反映。学生在这一语境中学习语言,不仅能更形象地学习词汇,而且愿学乐学,能在学习过程中更好地感悟体验生活。

其他教授词汇的方法还有同义词、反义词、词汇分类和上下义词等方法。英译汉翻译法的使用需要关注。一般来说,不建议在呈现词汇的词义时直接使用汉语翻译。但是不能一概而论,对于某些不适合用英语解释的抽象词汇使用汉语翻译法更加有效,易于理解。选择翻译法时应遵循"Speak English as possible, speak Chinese as necessary."的原则。

2. 练习词汇的活动

练习词汇的教学活动多种多样,但是万变不离其宗,总是围绕着一个目的设计活动,即练习词汇的"音、形、义、用"。

案例

活动名称:Look and match

活动意图:侧重词的形义练习。

活动内容:教师出示图片和单词,学生将图片和对应单词连线匹配。

**案例二**

活动名称：Listen and point

活动意图：侧重词的音义练习。

活动内容：教师出示图片,让学生推测图片意思。然后教师播放录音,学生根据所听到的单词指出对应图片。

**案例三**

活动名称：打地鼠

活动意图：侧重词的音形练习。

活动内容：本活动是 Listen and point 的变体。教师读单词,两生比赛,听音快速击打黑板上的单词图或文字。打地鼠活动也可以通过多媒体课件实现。

案例四

活动名称：The odd one out/Which is different?

活动意图：侧重词的音义或者形义练习,同时训练学生发散思维和逻辑思维能力。

活动内容：学生从四张图片中选出哪一个与其他三个不是一类,说出图片对应的单词。此活动的变换形式还可以是,教师写或者说一组单词,学生找出不同类的一个。

三、教学片段模拟训练

片段一

PEP《英语(三年级起点)》三年级上册 Unit 3 Look at me!中的 Let's learn

Situation: Art Room

1. T: Look! Say hello to Mickey! This is a face. Read after me—face ...

    S: ...

2. T: Look! Say hello to Tu Tu! This is an ear. Read after me—ear ...

S: ...

3. T: Listen, who is singing? Yes, the cute yellow Minions spring up a big surprise. Say hello to them! This is an eye. Read after me—eye ...

   S: ...

4. T: Look! Say hello to Pinocchio! This is a nose. Read after me—nose ...

   S: ...

5. T: Look! Say hello to SpongeBob! This is a mouth. Read after me—mouth ...

   S: ...

【设计意图】本课的新授词汇是 ear, eye, nose, mouth 和 face。教师选取了著名卡通人物,利用其有特色的面部特征呈现新知词汇。将创设的多个系列情境与参观艺术教室相互联系起来,避免情境的零散性和随意性,实现了教学情境的整体性和连贯性,有助于教学内容的自然过渡和衔接。

案例视频

(练习者:张瑶瑶)

片段二

PEP《英语(三年级起点)》三年级上册 Unit 3 Look at me! 中的 Let's learn

T: Look at me, please! What's this? (Teacher points at her own eye)

Ss: ...

T: Eye. Read after me. Eye. Open your mouth like this. Eye. Eye ... One eye is an eye, two eyes are eyes (Teacher points at her own eyes), read after me, eyes, eyes.

T: Look at me, please! What's this? (Teacher points at her own ear)

Ss: ...

T: Ear. Read after me. Ear. E says /ɪ/. Ear. Ear ... One ear is an ear, two ears are ears (Teacher points at her own ears), read after me, ears, ears.

T: Look at me, please! What's this? (Teacher points at her own nose)

Ss: ...

T: Nose. Read after me. Nose. Se says /z/. Nose. Nose. Touch your nose!

T: Look at me, please! What's this? (Teacher points at her own mouth)

Ss: ...

T: Mouth. Read after me. Mouth. Th says /θ/. Mouth. Mouth. Touch your mouth!

T: Look at me, please! What's this? (Teacher points at her own face)

Ss: ...

T: Face. Read after me. Face. Face. Touch your face!

【设计意图】本课新授词汇有关人的五官,这些器官每个人都有。结合词汇的这一特点,教师使用了最省时省力的直观呈现,既有利于学生建立词汇音形义之间的联系,又有助于激发学习兴趣。

案例视频

(练习者:王玲新)

四、范例导读

课文来源

PEP《英语（三年级起点）》六年级上册 Unit 2 Ways to go to school

单元整体设计

（一）教材内容

课文内容

（二）单元教学内容与要求

主题模块	学习内容		学习水平	学习与评价要求
1 语音	1.1　读音规则	1.1.1　英语句子中单词之间的连读现象	A	知晓英语句子中单词之间的连读现象
2 词汇	2.1　核心词汇：on foot, by bus, by plane, by taxi, by ship, by subway, by train, slow down, go, stop		C	背记、理解与运用 on foot, by bus, by plane, by taxi, by ship, by subway, by train, slow down, go, stop
3 词法	3.1　动词	3.1.1　实义动词	B	理解实义动词的祈使语气
		3.1.2　情态动词	A	知晓情态动词 must 必须与行为动词（原形）一起表达完整的意思
	3.2　介词	3.2.1　表示地点的介词	A	知晓介词 at 表示在……附近、旁边
4 句法	4.1　祈使句	4.1.1　表示命令、叮嘱、号召的祈使句	C	理解、运用表示命令、叮嘱、号召的祈使句
		4.1.2　表示建议的祈使句	C	理解、运用表示建议的祈使句
		4.1.3　祈使句的语调	B	理解在表示请求和命令时，祈使句一般用降调
5 语篇	5.1　记叙文	5.1.1　基本信息 Read and write	B	获取并简单讲述短文中的时间、地点、人物、事件等基本信息
		5.1.1　基本信息 Story time	A	简单讲述对话中的时间、地点、人物、事件等基本信息

备注：A 知晓　B 理解　C 运用

（三）单元教学与评价目标

1. 语言运用目标

学生能在 Go to school 和 Ask the way 的语境中,借助图片和文字,运用核心词汇 on foot, by bus, by plane, by taxi, by ship, by subway, by train, slow down, go, wait, stop 等及核心句型 How do you come/go to school? I usually/often/sometimes come/go on foot/… 谈论交通方式。用 Don't …You/I must… 来谈论交通规则,给同伴或自己提出安全出行的建议,同时能仿照范例绘制自己的交通规则海报。做到语音语调正确、优美,语意表达较有逻辑,拼写和语法正确。

2. 知识技能目标

（1）学生能知晓英语句子中单词之间连读的现象。

（2）学生能在语境中知晓、理解、背记并运用核心词汇 on foot, by bus, by plane, by taxi, by ship, by subway, by train, slow down, go, wait, stop 谈论或描述交通方式和交通规则,并能正确书写。

（3）学生能在语境中理解并运用核心句型 How do you come to school? Usually, I come on foot 询问和表达出行方式;用 In the USA people on bikes must wear helmet. Don't …You/I must… 来谈论交通规则,给同伴或自己提出安全出行的建议,同时能仿照范例绘制自己的交通规则海报。

（4）学生能在语境中听懂、读懂语篇并提取相关信息,能够按照正确的意群及语音、语调朗读故事,并运用本单元所学核心句型复述故事,同时能够根据阅读所获信息写出故事梗概。

（5）学生能通过看图捕捉主要信息,并根据提示做出听前预测;能够通读文段,获取主旨大意和细节信息,并能进行推理判断。

3. 文化意识目标

（1）了解不同国家学生上学的交通方式。

（2）能够辨认一些常见的交通标志,了解并遵守交通规则。

（3）知道英国和中国驾驶习惯的差异。

（四）分课时教学与评价目标

课时与板块	知识与技能	语用与情感	评价活动
第一课时 P14 Let's try Let's talk	1. 能读懂题目要求,在听前预测听力重点,能运用听力技巧完成听力任务 2. 能理解、朗读并背记核心词汇 on foot, by bus, by car, by bike 3. 能感知、理解、正确朗读并书写核心句型 How do you come to school? Usually, I come on foot. 简单询问和回答交通方式 4. 能在语境中感知、理解对话内容并能模仿读演对话	1. 能在语境中借助图文模仿读演对话,做到语言基本正确、表达比较流利并且有一定情感 2. 在谈论来某地的交通方式的语境中,运用核心语言,对自己喜爱的出行方式进行口头介绍,语音语调准确、内容完整达意、表达流利	1. 根据提示完成表格并用本课核心句型与词汇采访并概括自己同伴和老师来学校的交通方式 2. 根据图文提示运用本课核心句型与词汇介绍自己最喜欢的交通方式并简单阐述理由

（续表）

课时与板块	知识与技能	语用与情感	评价活动
第二课时 P15 Let's learn Write and say	1. 能理解、朗读并书写核心词汇on foot, by bus, by taxi, by plane, by subway, by train, by ship 2. 能在语境下正确使用Let's...表达建议；正确使用How do we get to ...? By...询问出行方式并回答	能简单表达去不同目的地的交通方式	1. 根据图片提示的情境,准确、连贯地表达去不同地方的交通方式 2. 根据图片提示的情境,运用核心词汇准确写目的地和出行方式
第三课时 P16 Let's try Let's talk	1. 能读懂题目要求,在听前预测听力重点,能运用听力技巧完成听力任务 2. 能理解、朗读并运用词汇go, get to, pay attention, 核心句Don't ...You/I must...来谈论交通规则,给同伴或自己提出安全出行的建议 3. 能在语境中感知、理解对话内容并能模仿读演对话 4. 通过对话学习了解欧美国家骑自行车的注意事项,了解不同的交通警示标志和这些标志出现的场所	1. 能在语境中借助图文模仿读演对话,做到语言基本正确,表达比较流利并且有一定情感 2. 能给同伴或自己提出安全出行的建议 3. 能遵守交通规则	1. 根据课文情景表演对话 2. 简单说出不同的交通警示标志和这些标志出现的场所
第四课时 P17 Let's learn Role-play	1. 能在语境中理解、朗读并书写核心词汇slow down, stop, wait, go 2. 能用We/You must...来提出合理建议,并能正确书写该句型	能模拟不同交通信号灯下行人和车辆的通行方式	根据提示模拟不同交通信号灯下行人和车辆的通行方式
第五课时 P18-P19 Read and write Tips for pronunciation	1. 能通过头脑风暴汇总已知的上学方式,激活已有的背景知识和储备词汇 2. 能够在阅读训练中捕捉关键信息和细节信息,提炼出文章的主旨大意 3. 能根据示范的海报完成安全海报的设计 4. 能根据例句提示在文段中找到更多同类现象,能正确朗读句子和语篇 5. 能知晓英语句子中单词之间连读的现象	能根据示范的海报完成安全海报的设计	1. 根据示范的海报完成安全海报的设计 2. 找出本课语篇中单词间连读的地方
第六课时 P20-P21 Story time Let's check Let's wrap it up	1. 能通过阅读趣味故事,知晓英国和中国驾驶习惯的差异 2. 能正确完成听力练习 3. 知晓、了解实意动词come和go在句子中表达的不同语义	能知晓英国和中国驾驶习惯的差异	小组合作表演故事,简单介绍英国和中国驾驶习惯的差异

课时教学设计

PEP《英语(三年级起点)》六年级上册 Unit 2 Ways to go to school中的 Let's learn

【设 计 者】济南市长清区石麟小学　林倩倩

【案例说明】

本单元重点学习如何询问和回答人们日常出行的方式,这个话题与学生的日常生活紧密联系。这一单元分主情景图,A,B和C三部分,A部分主要包含 Let's try, Let's talk, Let's learn, Write and say四个环节。主要学习日常出行方式,呈现基础知识。在学习单词过程中自然地将教学重点引到语言运用上来。B部分主要包含 Let's try, Let's talk, Let's learn, Role-play, Read and write, Let's check, Let's wrap it up七个环节。主要介绍常用的交通规则、交通标志以及各地学生上学的方式。C部分只有Story time一个环节。主要是综合前两部分所学知识,以故事的形式复习知识,同时介绍部分中西方文化差异。

通过本单元的学习,使学生能够正确询问并回答乘坐某种交通工具去某地,能够描述人们日常出行的方式,并简单陈述理由。帮助学生了解交通规则,教育学生在生活中自觉遵守交通规则,同时让学生体会到现代交通方式的便捷。

本课时作为单元的第二课时,生词量较少,语法知识相对简单。主要任务是让学生能够熟练使用所学语言询问并回答乘坐某种交通工具去某地,其核心句型为: How do you go to ...? I go ... on foot/by bus/train在教学中,教师应充分利用旧知识为新知识的教学服务,尽可能多地创设情境为学生提供运用语言的机会。通过创设情境,使新词不断涌出。整合文本,引导学生复述。为了拓展、丰富学生的语言,让英语更贴近生活,最后呈现了一篇拓展阅读,培养学生运用语言的能力。

【教学流程】

Warm up and lead-in	·Free talk ·Sing a song
Presentation and practice	·Situation 1:(1) Listen and answer (2) Present "taxi" (3) Listen and imitate (4) Role play ·Situation 2:(1) Listen and answer (2) Listen and fill (3) Listen and answer (4) Listen and choose 　　　　　　(5) Retell (6) Route design
Consolidation	·Read and underline ·Travel plan ·Video
Homework	·Talk about your ways to go somewhere ·Read picture books about transportation

【教学设计】

一、教学目标

1. 能听、说、读、写词组：by plane/by train/by taxi/by ship/on foot/by bus/by subway。

2. 能正确使用上述短语谈论交通方式，并能听、说、认读句型：How do you go to school? How do you go to work? I go ...

3. 通过学习，使学生感受到现代交通方式的便捷，体会到The convenient transportation makes our world a big family。

二、教学重难点

1. 重点：听、说、读、写词组by plane/by train/by taxi/by ship/on foot/by bus/by subway及谈论出行方式。

2. 难点：根据现实情况选择并谈论出行方式。

三、教具准备

图片、单词卡、视频、PPT

四、教学过程

Teaching steps	Teachers' activities	Students' activities

I. Warm-up and lead-in	1. Self-introduction.
	   T: Hello, my name is Daisy. I am an English teacher. I like playing sports. I often go to work on foot.
	2. I am a teacher. I go to school on foot. You are students. How do you go to school? By car, by bike or by bus?
	3. Pair work.
	   A: How do you go to school?
	   B: I go to school _____.
	4. Sing a song: How do you come to school?
		Answer the questions.
		Do the pair work.
		Sing a song.

II. Presentation and practice	1. Situation 1:
	   T: Mrs. Smith is going to take her children to the nature park.
	   (1) Listen and answer.
	   T: How do they get there? Do they get there by bus, by car or by taxi?
	   (2) Present "taxi".
	   T: Look! This is a taxi. Taxi ... Let's read it one by one. Very good! "By taxi", "by taxi".
	   (3) Listen and imitate.
	   (4) Role play.
	2. Situation 2:
	   T: I will introduce a friend to you. Look! Who is she? ... We will meet Ann's family.
	
	Hello, I'm Ann.
	I'm a student.
	I go to school on foot.
		Listen and answer the questions.
		
		Students read: *by taxi*
		
		Listen and imitate.
		Role play.

Teaching steps	Teachers' activities	Students' activities
II. Presentation and practice	Hello, I'm Ann's Dad. I work in a bank. I go to work by subway. Hello, I'm Ann's mum. I work in a hospital. I often go to work by car, sometimes I go by taxi. Hello, we are Ann's grandparents. We often go travelling by train, sometimes we go by ship or by plane. (1) Listen and answer. 图片一一呈现出 Ann 的家人。 T: How do they go to school/go to work/...? 回归到文本内容，Listen and imitate. T: They have different ways. How does Ann go to school? Let's listen. (2) Listen and fill. （出示爸爸的图片）T: Look! This is Ann's dad, and he is a bank clerk. How does he go to work? Let's listen and fill. Present and practice "by subway" and "Good to know". (3) Listen and answer. 图片一一呈现出 Ann 的家人，学生听录音，整体感知文本内容。 T: How does her mum go to work? Let's listen. Present and practice "*by taxi*". (4) Listen and choose. 　　T: Ann's grandparents like traveling. How do they go travelling? Listen and choose. 　　Present and practice "*by ship, by plane, by train*".	Listen and answer the questions. Listen and imitate. Listen and fill. Students learn and practice: *by subway* Listen and imitate. Students learn and practice: *Good to know* Listen and answer the questions. Students practice: *by taxi* Listen and imitate. Students listen and choose the answer: We usually go travelling by train, sometimes we go by ship or by plane. Listen and imitate.

（续表）

Teaching steps	Teachers' activities	Students' activities
II. Presentation and practice	(5) Retell. (6) Let's practice—route design. （出示地图）T: How do you get to Dalian from Yantai? How do you get to Seoul from Jinan? How do you get to Shanghai from Beijing?	Students retell according to the table. Students choose the proper way of transportation.
III. Consolidation	1. Read and underline. 　T: How do you get there? 2. Group work. Write your travel plan. 3. Present a video— 　Transportation in the future. T: The convenient transportation makes our world a big family.	Students read the two passages and underline the way of transportation. Students write their travel plan. Students watch a video.

（续表）

Teaching steps	Teachers' activities	Students' activities
IV. Homework	1. Talk about your ways to go somewhere. 2. Read picture books about transportation.   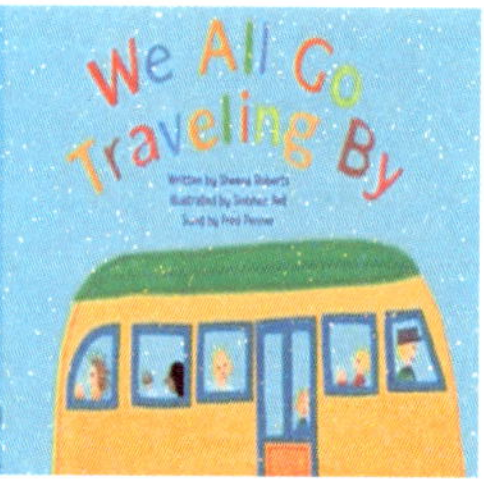	
Blackboard Design		

【设计思路】

本课的主题是出行方式。具体教学内容为对常见出行方式 by plane/by train/by taxi/ by ship/on foot/by bus/by subway 等短语和对句式结构 How do you go to school? How do you go to work? I go...的学习。设计者通过自由会话辅以思维导图的方式介绍自己。通过兴趣爱好 sports，自然过渡到 go to work on foot，再通过问答 I am a teacher. I go to school on foot. You are students. How do you go to school?将话题引到所学主题——出行方式。本课教学中，设计者使用了多种方式呈现和巩固新知。通过声音、图像、视频等媒体方式，让学生感知各种出行方式的特点。在授课的过程中，让新词不断地涌出、推进，使之逐渐地学习。使用图片直观呈现了新知 by bus。使用课本情境教授了 by taxi。创设了情境 Ann's family，利用四幅图片一一呈现出 Ann 的家人，学生听录音，整体感知文本内容。每一个人物的出场，不同的人物声音有所变化，通过听录音，学生明白 They have different ways。通过对家庭成员不同出行方式的介绍，教授了 by subway 等新知，并练习巩固了已学知识。练习的形式从机械性的跟读仿说到根据图表提示复述 Ann 一家人的出行方式，再到根据地图选择合适的交通方式，解决真实生活中的问题。练习的设计兼顾了层次性与递进性。巩固提高阶段，由两个活动组成。第一个活动使用了阅读后介绍这种形式，培养学生综合语言运用能力。第二部分播放了一个介绍未来出行方式的视频,让大家体会到便捷的出行方式,让我们的世界成为一个大家庭。

五、课后训练

根据PEP《英语(三年级起点)》三年级上册Unit 3 Look at me! 中的Let's learn部分,撰写一份教学设计并试讲。

- 了解会话教学的功能
- 识别会话教学内容
- 运用常用教学方法组织教学
- 教学设计关注会话的"主题语境、核心语言、情感表达、文化渗透"

一、会话教学概述

　　会话教学也称对话教学,它是小学英语课堂教学的重要组成部分。小学阶段的英语学习,尤其是中低段,内容大多以对话的形式呈现。会话教学主要是培养学生口头表达能力和交际能力,提高会话技巧,提升"用英语做事情"的能力。交际性和互动性是会话课区别于其他课型的重要特征。会话教学的教学目标是要让学生在理解文本的基础上,能够运用目标句型在具体的情景中开展对话。教师要引导学生通过听、读、演等各种操练活动为"说"做铺垫,让学生逐渐掌握和运用相应的语言项目,并就特定的话题展开交流,为形成初步的交流能力打下基础。

　　目前各个版本的教材都是以会话为核心内容进行编排的。如PEP《英语(三年级起点)》(人民教育出版社)中的Let's talk部分,《英语(牛津上海版)》(上海教育出版社)中的Look and say部分,《英语(三年级起点)》(外语教学与研究出版社)中Listen, read and act out部分,都是专门针对会话进行学习的板块。以PEP《英语(三年级起点)》(人民教育出版社)六年级下册中的 Unit 1 中的 Let's talk 部分为例，内容为在参观恐龙博物馆的语境中比较并描述人、动物的外貌特征。

　　会话教学主要关注会话的"主题语境、核心语言、情感表达、文化渗透"四个方面。主题语境是会话教学的必备条件。语言习得只有在真实的语境中才能产生。只有了解会话发生的主题语境，才能更准确地运用语言进行交际。教师可以利用课本插图、引入生活情境或者创设接近真实的主题语境帮助学生理解会话内容。核心语言是会话文本中的核心词语和核心句型，包括语音、词汇、语法以及用于表达话题和功能的语言形式。核心语言一定要放在主题语境中教学，聚焦核心词句的语音语调和语流语速。可以通过 Shadow reading 的方式训练语音语调和语流语速。会话的功能是交换信息和表情达意，通过语言来表达情感。教师可以设计有趣的配音游戏或者角色扮演活动来训练情感表达。会话文本中有丰富的文化内涵。在会话教学中，教师要关注语言和语用中的文化因素，引导学生了解和比较中外文化的异同，帮助他们逐步形成跨文化交际能力。

二、常用教学方法与活动

　　会话教学活动多种多样，但是都紧紧围绕着既定话题，运用核心语言来实施，最终目标指向让学生爱说、敢说、会说。

1. Warm-up 启动——激发兴趣　激活已知

　　通常我们在热身环节采用听、说、做、唱、演等形式，借助有趣的歌曲、歌谣、游戏、谜语、动作等资源，激发学生学习英语的兴趣，激活学生已有的知识经验，使其快速融入英语学习的氛围。例如：《英语（牛津上海版）》四年级上册 Module 2 Unit 2 中的 Listen and enjoy 部分就可以用作本单元会话课的热身活动。

活动名称：Listen and do

活动意图：激发兴趣，激活学生已有的知识经验，为学习新知做铺垫。

活动内容：教师播放歌谣，学生一边听音跟说一边做出相应动作。

> **Jobs**
> **Listen and enjoy**
> Look at the fire,
> Fire, fire, fire!
> Call the fire station,
> One, one, nine!
> Bring the fire engine,
> Engine, engine, engine!
> The brave firefighters
> Put out the fire!
>
> 22

2. Presentation 呈现——创设情境　整体输入

在情境中整体呈现会话内容。教师充分利用教材情境、引入真实情境或者创设接近真实的语言情境,把对话中的核心词句、语法融入具体的、有意义的情境中,整体呈现给学生,通过提问、实物、动作等帮助学生理解,体会情感,内化语言,最终促进学生综合语用能力的发展。会话教学关键是让学生在理解对话语篇的基础上学习语言,这样语言才会真实和鲜活。在教学中,教师的任何活动都是围绕会话的情境进行的。这样学生不仅理解了其含义,还学会了如何运用。

以PEP《英语(三年级起点)》五年级下册Unit 2 What's your favorite season? 为例,在呈现会话时可以充分利用课本插图来解读主题语境。教材中插图的功能首先是阐释语境,教师自身首先要认真研读插图,借助观察、讨论等多种手段分析图意,引导学生观察、解读主题语境,使隐藏信息充分展现出来,使学生体验并理解真实的语义,提高口语表达的真实性。

师生展开对话如下:

T: Look at the picture. Who are they?

Ss: They are Mr Jones, Mike and Wu Binbin.

T: Where are they? What are they talking about?

S1: They are in the classroom. They are talking about seasons.

S2: Mike says "I like winter." Wu Binbin says "I like spring".

T: Why are they talking about seasons? Are they having an English class?

Ss: No, they aren't. They are having an art class. Mr Jones is an art teacher.

T: Why are they talking about seasons in an art class?

Ss: Maybe they just want to draw the seasons.

T: OK. That's reasonable. Let's watch and think about how they have the art class.

Ss: At first, they listen to music. Then they draw pictures.

T: Which season does Mike like best? Which season does Wu Binbin like best? And Mr Jones?

Let's listen to the whole dialogue and find out the answers.

3. Practice 操练——多法并举　突破重点

在会话的操练环节我们可以采用影子跟读、游戏、创编歌谣或歌曲等多种方法来突破核心词句和处理细节词句。操练的目的是提高学生语音语调、语流语速和情感表达的准确性和流畅性。在操练环节切记要在大语境下多进行意义操练和交际性训练,减少枯燥的机械操练。

案例二

活动名称:Shadowing 影子跟读

活动意图:在影子跟读训练中,听觉、视觉、语言几种模态协同运作,有效集中学生注意力,锻炼学生辨别语音的能力,有效提高学生口语的准确度。

活动内容:教师播放语音材料,学生尽可能在听到声音的同时清晰地读出语音。学生的跟读只比原材料延后一两秒,而且要保持内容和语音、语调与所听材料一致。

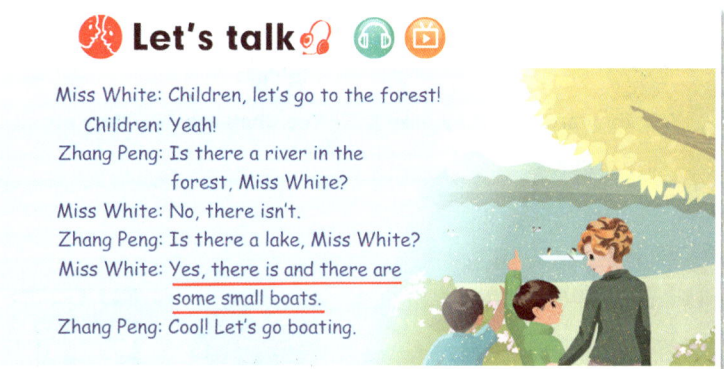

Let's talk

Miss White: Children, let's go to the forest!
Children: Yeah!
Zhang Peng: Is there a river in the forest, Miss White?
Miss White: No, there isn't.
Zhang Peng: Is there a lake, Miss White?
Miss White: Yes, there is and there are some small boats.
Zhang Peng: Cool! Let's go boating.

Step 1: Listen to the tape and repeat what you hear as soon as you hear it.
　　　　边听边看课本边跟读全文,争取做到与课文录音同时同步。

Step 2: Underline the sentences that you couldn't shadow well.
　　　　标出跟不上的句子。

Step 3: Shadow the sentences only.
　　　　反复跟读这个跟不上的句子。

Step 4: Shadow the whole dialogue again.
　　　　再次跟读全文。

案例三

活动名称:Guessing game

活动意图:让学生在真实语境中运用核心词句做事情,突破重点。

活动内容:学生用核心词句进行问答,玩游戏。在有趣的游戏中学生突破重点或难点词句的学习,在玩中学。

例如：会话文本的核心句型是 Are they ...? Yes, they are. No, they aren't. 教师设计了 Look and guess 的问答游戏。借助多媒体课件分层呈现图片内容，引导学生运用核心句型进行问答游戏。

案例四

活动名称：Let's wave! 人浪游戏
活动意图：突破难点长句朗读。
活动内容：将长句分解，让学生分组起立朗读，几组同学合作完成长句的朗读。

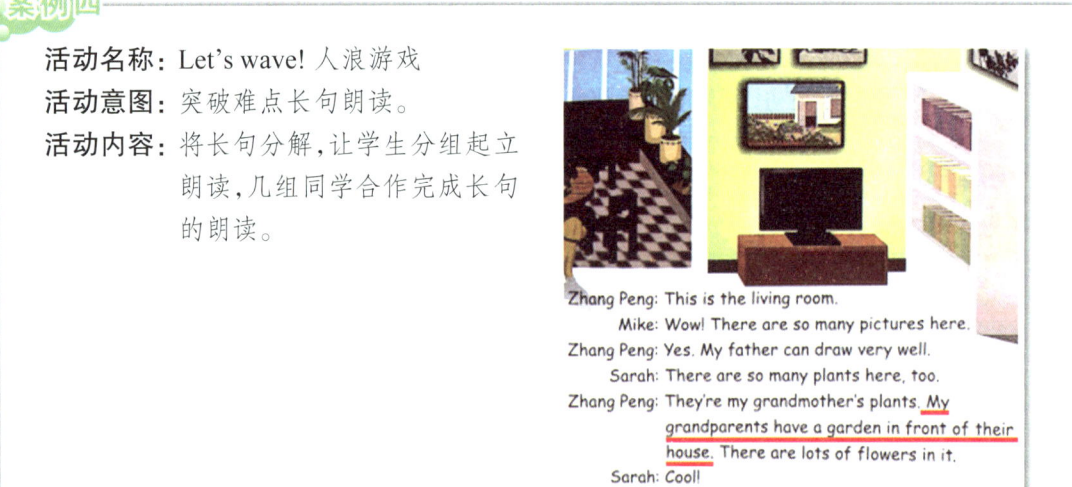

Zhang Peng: This is the living room.
Mike: Wow! There are so many pictures here.
Zhang Peng: Yes. My father can draw very well.
Sarah: There are so many plants here, too.
Zhang Peng: They're my grandmother's plants. My grandparents have a garden in front of their house. There are lots of flowers in it.
Sarah: Cool!

例如，在教授 PEP《英语（三年级起点）》五年级上册 Unit 5 Part B Let's talk 中的长句子 My grandparents have a garden in front of their house. 时，教师采用将长句按意群分解的方式，把学生分成三组，每组认领一个词组，一组 My grandparents，二组 have a garden，三组 in front of their house，以人浪的方式起立接龙朗读，将词组连成一句。期间可以不断变换各组词组的顺序，让学生在视觉、听觉、动觉等多感官协同运作下，突破长句朗读中的连读、重读和停顿。

案例五

活动名称: Role-play 角色扮演

活动意图: 为学生提供大量语言实践的机会,提高学生主动说英语的积极性,提高课堂参与度,提高学习效率。

活动内容: 教师引导学生先视听课文,充分练习后请学生进行角色扮演,重现对话内容或创造性改编对话内容进行表演。注意这里的表演指的是脱稿表演,不仅不能看词,还需要注意表情、动作和现场互动。教师可以引导学生参照这样的表演范式:

Step 1. Self-introduction

Step 2. Role playing

Step 3. Curtain call

在小组合作排练完毕后,组长找老师"约号",先准备好的小组可以成功预约 1 号,之后依次类推。准备时间结束时,按照学生所约的顺序,逐一进行对话的表演。

在教授 PEP《英语(三年级起点)》五年级上册 Unit 4 中的 Let's talk 时,引导学生根据自己的实际改编对话并表演。学生表演片段如下:

(一名学生扮演本级部的体育刘老师,四名学生扮演真实的自己,其中 Kevin 是学校武术队成员。)

Mr Liu: Good afternoon, children. Today we'll learn some kung fu.

Children: Cool!

Mr Liu: Can you do any kung fu, Kevin?(拍 Kevin 肩膀)

Kevin: Yes, I can.(武术姿势亮相)

Mr Liu: Wonderful!(竖起大拇指)

(转头问其余三人)Can you do any kung fu?

Children: No, we can't.(摆手摇头)

Mr Liu: No problem. Kevin and I can help you.

One, two, three!

（学生列队站好，Mr Liu 和 Kevin 在前排喊着口号教三个武术动作，其余学生边喊边跟做。此表演受到现场学生观众的热烈追捧，纷纷在台下跟着说跟着做。）

小学生的活泼好动、喜爱表现、愿意接受挑战等特点决定了他们非常喜爱这样的表演活动。在表演过程中，学生把会话文本这种单一的文字模态，转化为自己的声音、动作、表情等模态，强化了对文本的理解和记忆，在创造性改编对话的过程中，还提高了用语言表达自己心理和情绪的能力。学生在 pair work 或 group work 中获得了更多的练习机会，并及时从同伴处获得反馈信息，口语交流效率提高。

4. Production 拓展——基于文本　超越文本

拓展不是让学生照搬会话中的词句完成表演，而是让学生在小组内运用所学核心词句围绕话题在特定的任务或者语境中进行交际。在会话课的拓展环节，教师可以设计真实的、贴近生活的任务帮助学生实际运用语言。

例如：《英语（三年级起点）》（外语教学与研究出版社）五年级下册 Module 4 中的 Unit 1 的主题是 Let's make a home library。在学习、操练并表演课本对话后，教师可以设计一个 Let's make a classroom library 的拓展任务。引导学生利用本班教室的图书和橱柜，以四人小组的形式，运用本节课的核心词句来交流，完成建立教室图书馆的任务。

三、教学片段模拟训练

片段一

新起点《英语（一年级起点）》六年级上册 Unit 2 **Around the world** 中的 **Look, listen and say.**

Warm-up（启动环节）

1. Free talk.

T: Good afternoon, boys and girls. Look here, where is China? Yes, it's in the east of Asia. It's our motherland. It's famous for the Great Wall and giant panda. We Chinese people speak Chinese. There are many other countries in the world, such as the USA ...

S1: UK.

S2: Canada.

T: Well done.

【设计意图】教师通过展示地球仪，引导学生们在地图上找到自己的国家，并谈论中国的特色。在自由交谈中营造轻松的开课氛围，激发学习兴趣。

2. Brain storming.

Let's look and say quickly. What country is this?

Ss: USA, UK, Australia ...

【设计意图】头脑风暴活动中，根据国家特色景物或者事物快速辨别国家，学生的思维和已有的知识经验被激活。

Lesson 2

A Look, listen and say.
1. What countries and cities can you see on the map?
2. Now listen and say.

Miss Wu: Boys and girls, look at the map please. What country is this?
Bill: It's Canada.
Miss Wu: What do you know about Canada?
Bill: Canada is a big country. It's famous for maple leaves. They are beautiful. People there speak English and French. Toronto is a very big city. It's in the southeast of Canada. You can visit the CN Tower there.
Miss Wu: Good. What about this country? What do you know about it?
Joy: This is Australia. It's famous for koalas and kangaroos. They are cute. People there speak English. Sydney is in the southeast of Australia. The Opera House there is famous.
Miss Wu: Well done.

案例视频

（济南市经五路小学　王　冠）

片段二

PEP《英语（三年级起点）》六年级上册 Unit 6 **How do you feel?** 中的 **Let's talk**

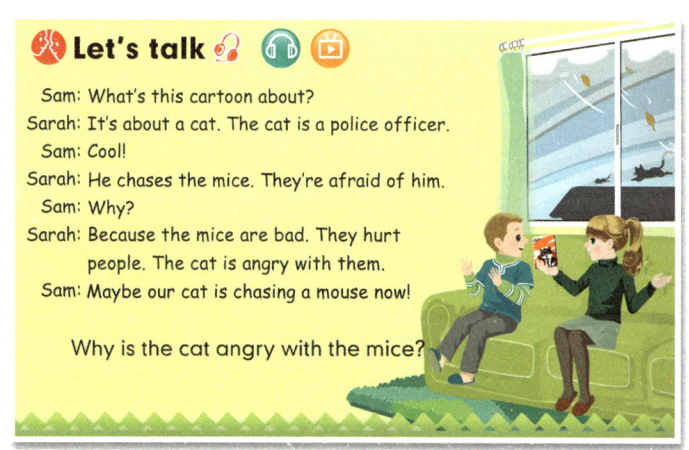

Let's talk

Sam: What's this cartoon about?
Sarah: It's about a cat. The cat is a police officer.
Sam: Cool!
Sarah: He chases the mice. They're afraid of him.
Sam: Why?
Sarah: Because the mice are bad. They hurt people. The cat is angry with them.
Sam: Maybe our cat is chasing a mouse now!

Why is the cat angry with the mice?

Practice（操练环节）

1. Listen and imitate.

   T: Let's read and imitate the dialogue.

2. Shadow reading.

   T: Let's read the dialogue while listening.

3. Read and act in roles.

   T: OK, who can read it?

   Students raise their hands.

   T: (choose one and ask) Can you be Sam? Please choose *Sarah* yourself.

   Then two students read the dialogue in roles.

   T: Please work in pairs. One is Sarah, and the other one is Sam. You will have one minute.

4. Let's sing.

   Cat, cat. Cool, cool, cool!

   He chases the mice.

   Mice, mice. Bad, bad, bad.

   They're afraid of him.

   The mice are bad.

   The mice are bad.

   The cat is angry with them.

   The mice are bad.

   The mice are bad.

   La la la la   la la la.

   The mice are bad.

【设计意图】操练环节运用了四步递进的方式来引导学生操练对话。通过听音模仿、影子跟读、角色表演和创编歌曲唱出对话重难点，让学生在体验角色的同时达到主动运用语言的目的。通过一句接一句的听音模仿跟读可以训练学生的听辨能力，提高语音的准确性。借助影子跟读的形式训练学生的语速。在学生小组合作练习对话之前，教师一定要请学生代表进行合作示范，这样可以生动、具体地告知所有学生pair work如何进行。根据对话重点创编的歌曲可以帮助学生突破重点，为学生营造一种轻松愉悦的学习氛围，提高学生的兴趣，让他们愿意开口。借助音乐的旋律与歌词的韵律来培养学生的语感，激发学生各种潜能，有效调动各种感官对信息进行加工、整理，从而促进语言的内化、记忆和表达。

案例视频

（济南市经五路小学
王　冠）

四、范例导读

课 文 来 源

PEP《英语（三年级起点）》六年级上册 Unit 6 How do you feel?

单元整体设计

（一）教材内容

课文内容

（二）单元教学内容与要求

主题模块	学习内容		学习水平	学习与评价要求
1 语音	1.1　读音规则	1.1.1　英语句子中单词之间失去爆破的现象	A	知晓英语句子中单词之间失去爆破的现象
2 词汇	2.1　核心词汇：feel, sad, angry, happy, worried, afraid, wrong, ill, see the doctor, do more exercise, wear warm clothes, take a deep breath, count to ten		C	背记、理解与运用 feel, sad, angry, happy, worried, afraid, wrong, ill, see the doctor, do more exercise, wear warm clothes, take a deep breath, count to ten
3 词法	3.1　名词	3.1.1　可数名词复数的不规则变化	A	知晓可数名词复数的不规则变化
	3.2　形容词	3.2.1　形容词	A	知晓形容词在句中的表语、定语功能
	3.3　动词	3.3.1　情态动词	A	知晓情态动词必须与行为动词一起表达完整的意思
4 句法	4.1　句子种类	4.1.1　陈述句	C	用陈述句 The mice are afraid of the cat. The cat is angry with them. 等简单表达相关的情绪和心理状态。用 ... should ... 提出建议
		4.1.2　疑问句　4.1.2.1　特殊疑问句	C	用特殊疑问句 How do you feel? How does ... feel? 进行提问，并回答 I am .../ He/She is ...
		4.1.3　祈使句	C	用祈使句 Don't ... 来疏导情绪
5 语篇	5.1　记叙文	5.1.1　基本信息　Read and write	B	故事基本信息的获得和描述
		5.1.1　基本信息　Story time	A	简单讲述对话中的时间、地点、人物、事件等基本信息

备注：A 知晓　B 理解　C 运用

（三）单元教学与评价目标

1. 语言运用目标

学生能在At Sarah's home的语境中，借助图片和文字，运用核心词汇feel, sad, angry, happy, worried, afraid, wrong, ill, see the doctor, do more exercise, wear warm clothes, take a deep breath, count to ten等及核心句型... are afraid of ..., ... is angry with them. How does ... feel?简单表达相关的情绪和心理状态。用Don't ..., ... should ...来疏导情绪和提出建议。做到语音语调正确、优美，语意表达较有逻辑，拼写和语法正确。

2. 知识技能目标

（1）学生能知晓英语句子中单词之间失去爆破的现象。

（2）学生能在语境中知晓、理解，背记并运用核心词汇feel, sad, angry, happy, worried, afraid, wrong, ill, see the doctor, do more exercise, wear warm clothes, take a deep breath, count to ten简单表达相关的情绪和心理状态，并能正确书写。

（3）学生能在语境中理解并运用核心句型... are afraid of ..., ... is angry with them简单表达相关的情绪和心理状态；用How does ... feel?询问他人情绪和心理状态；用Don't ..., ... should ...来疏导情绪和提出建议，并能正确书写该句型。

（4）学生能在语境中听懂、读懂语篇并提取相关信息，能够按照正确的意群及语音、语调朗读故事，并运用本单元所学核心句型复述故事，同时能够根据阅读所获信息写出故事梗概。

（5）学生能简单介绍中国的卡通名片《黑猫警长》。

（6）学生能通过看图捕捉主要信息，并根据提示做出听前预测；能够通读文段，获取主旨大意和细节信息，并能进行推理判断。

3. 语言情感目标

学生能准确表达情感情绪；不以自我为中心，关心他人，为他人着想；不以貌取人，要知恩图报。

（四）分课时教学与评价目标

课时与板块	知识与技能	语用与情感	评价活动
第一课时 P58 Let's try Let's talk	1. 能读懂题目要求，在听前预测听力重点，能运用听力技巧完成听力任务 2. 能理解、朗读并背记核心词汇feel, sad, angry, happy, worried, afraid 3. 能感知、理解、正确朗读并书写核心句型... are afraid of ..., ... is angry with ...简单表达相关的情绪和心理状态 4. 能在语境中感知、理解对话内容并能模仿读演对话	1. 能在语境中借助图文模仿读演对话，做到语言基本正确，表达比较流利并且有一定情感 2. 在谈论自己喜爱的卡通的语境中，运用核心语言，对自己喜爱的卡通片进行口头介绍，语音语调准确、内容完整达意、表达流利	1. 根据提示补全句子并用本课核心句型与词汇简单介绍中国的卡通名片《黑猫警长》 2. 根据图文提示运用本课核心句型与词汇简单介绍自己最喜欢的卡通片并表达自己真实的情感体验

（续表）

课时与板块	知识与技能	语用与情感	评价活动
第二课时 P59 Let's learn Write and say	1. 能理解、朗读并书写核心词汇feel，sad，angry，happy，worried，afraid 2. 能在语境下正确使用be+happy/sad/...表达人和动物的情绪和心理状态	能表达不同情境下人和动物的情绪和心理状态	1. 根据图片提示的情境，准确、连贯地表达Sarah和cat的情绪和心理状态 2. 根据图片提示的情境，运用核心词汇准确写出图中人物或动物的情绪和心理状态
第三课时 P60 Let's try Let's talk	1. 能读懂题目要求，在听前预测听力重点，能运用听力技巧完成听力任务 2. 能理解、朗读并背记核心词汇wrong，ill，see the doctor，简单表达相关的情绪和心理状态 3. 能用How does ... feel? 询问他人情绪和心理状态；能在语境下正确使用Don't ...，...should ... 来疏导情绪和提出建议 4. 能在语境中感知，理解对话内容并能模仿读演对话	1. 能在语境中借助图文模仿读演对话，做到语言基本正确，表达比较流利并且有一定情感 2. 能疏导情绪和提出建议 3. 能不以自我为中心，关心他人，为他人着想	1. 根据课文情景给Sarah和Sam进行情绪疏导并提出合理建议 2. 根据图片提示给图中的小伙伴疏导情绪和提出合理建议
第四课时 P61 Let's learn Play card games	1. 能在语境中理解、朗读并书写核心词汇do more exercise, wear warm clothes, take a deep breath, count to ten 2. 能用You should ... 来提出合理建议，并能正确书写该句型	能针对不同情绪分别提出有针对性的建议来疏导他人的情绪	根据图片提示给Chen Jie, Wu Binbin, Mike和Oliver提出建议或疏导情绪
第五课时 P62-P63 Read and write Tips for pronunciation	1. 能通过绘制表情图复习情绪单词 2. 能够在语篇中捕捉不同类型的信息，提炼出文章的主旨大意，完成排序题 3. 能根据阅读所获取的信息完成故事缩写活动并能口头复述 4. 能根据例句提示在文段中找到更多同类现象，能正确朗读句子和语篇 5. 能知晓英语句子中单词之间失去爆破的现象	能不以貌取人，明白团结的力量以及应当助人为乐	1. 复述并表演Robin和Little ant的故事 2. 找出本课语篇中单词间失去爆破的地方
第六课时 P64-P65 Story time Let's check Let's wrap it up	1. 能通过阅读趣味故事，复习巩固表达感情的句型I'm ... 和提出建议的句型... should ...，Don't ...，增加语言的输入 2. 能正确完成听力练习 3. 知晓、了解feel后面可以接表示感受和感情的形容词	能体会到情感的变化对故事情节的推动作用	小组合作表演故事，根据图片和文字提示与小组成员分享即时心情

课时教学设计

PEP《英语(三年级起点)》六年级上册 Unit 6 How do you feel?中的 Let's talk

【设 计 者】济南市经五路小学　王冠

【教学流程】

I. Warm-up	II. Presentation	III. Practice	VI. Production	V. Homework
Look and say	Watch and answer Watch and find out Listen and repeat	Shadow reading Pair work Role-play	Introduce the cartoon *Mr Black* Introduce the cartoon *Tom and Jerry*	To get more information about your fovorite cartoon and try to introduce it in English

【教学设计】

一、教学目标

1. 能理解、朗读并背记核心词汇：feel，sad，angry，happy，worried，afraid。能感知、理解、正确朗读并书写核心句型 ... are afraid of ..., ... is angry with ...。

2. 能在听前预测重点,能运用听力技巧完成听力任务。

3. 能在语境中感知、理解对话内容并能借助图文模仿读演对话,做到语言基本正确,表达比较流利并且有一定情感。

4. 能在语境中运用核心语言,对卡通片进行口头介绍,做到语音语调准确、内容完整达意、表达流利。

5. 识别卡通片中角色的感受;比较《黑猫警长》和《猫和老鼠》猫鼠角色的异同。

二、教学重难点

1. 重点:能在语境中借助图文模仿读演对话。

2. 难点:chases的发音;能在语境中运用核心语言,对卡通片进行口头介绍。

三、教具准备

PPT、视频、图卡

四、教学过程

Teaching steps	Teachers' activities	Students' activities
I. Warm-up	Look and say. Guide the students to review the words and sentences about 5 feelings. Such as happy, sad, angry, worried and afraid.	Students watch the screen and try to say the words and sentences loudly.

Teaching steps	Teachers' activities	Students' activities
II. Presentation	Let's talk. 1. T: Do you like cartoons? Sarah and Sam are going to watch a cartoon. Guide them to think about a question: What's this cartoon about? → Watch the video and find out the answer. → It's about a cat. T: What does he do? → The cat is a police officer. Ask the students to read it one by one. → mouse mice 2. Ask the students to watch the video again and try to find out: The cat is _____. The mice are _____ of him. → The cat is angry. → The mice are afraid of him. → WHY is the cat angry with the mice? → Because the mice are bad. They hurt people.	Think and answer. Watch the video and find out the answer. → It's about a cat. Students: The cat is a police officer. Students practice the sentences one by one. Learn the words mouse and mice. They try to describe the cat's feeling and the mouse's feeling. Watch the cartoon again and try to find out: The cat is _____. The mice are _____ of him. → The cat is angry. → The mice are afraid of him. → Students: Because the mice are bad. They hurt people.
III. Practice	1. Listen and imitate. 2. Shadow reading. Ask them to read with the video. 3. Read and act in roles. Practice the dialogue in pairs, and then show it. 4. Let's sing. *Cat, cat. Cool, cool, cool!* *He chases the mice.* *Mice, mice. Bad, bad, bad.* *They're afraid of him.* *The mice are bad.* *The mice are bad.* *The cat is angry with them.* *The mice are bad.* *The mice are bad.* *La la la la la la la.* *The mice are bad.*	Listen and imitate Students pay attention to these words: *chases* and *chasing*. Shadow reading They work in pairs, and then show it. Students sing the song.
IV. Production	1. Ask the students to introduce the cartoon *Mr Black*. 2. Ask the students to introduce another cartoon about cat and mouse: *Tom and Jerry*. 3. Ask the students to talk about their favorite cartoons.	Students introduce the cartoon *Mr Black* in English. Student introduces another cartoon about cat and mouse: *Tom and Jerry*. Students talk about their favorite cartoons.

（续表）

Teaching steps	Teachers' activities	Students' activities
V. Homework	To get more information about your favorite cartoon and try to introduce it in English.	
Blackboard Design	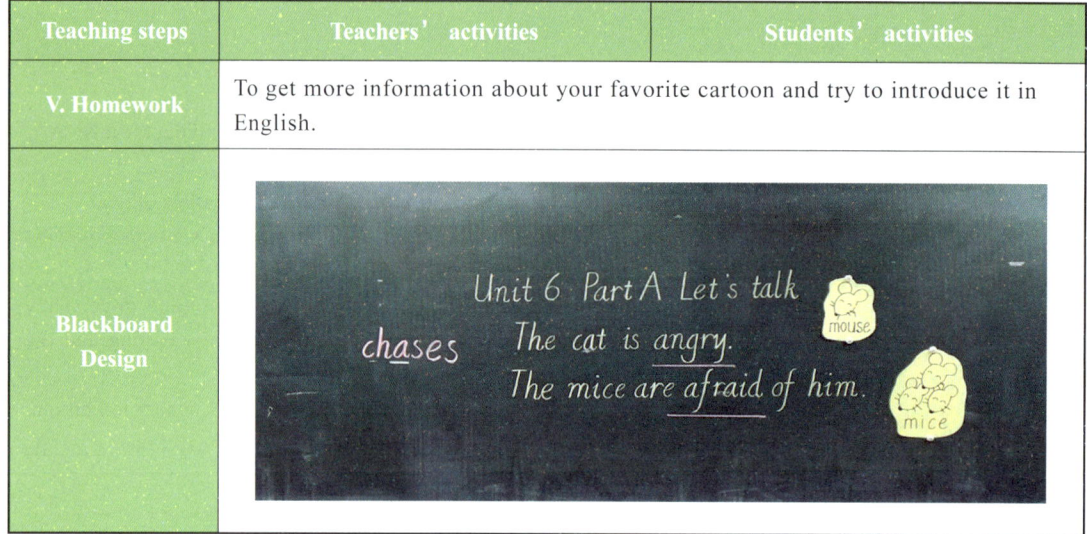	

【设计思路】

本课的主题是feelings，文本形式为对话。设计者主要按照以下三步来处理对话文本。第一步，导入话题，感知对话文本；第二步，分步突破，解读对话文本；第三步，实际运用，提升对话文本。首先，教师以快节奏视听读的方式热身并引出核心词汇。紧接着引入课文情景，让学生带着问题What's this cartoon about?来观看无字幕版视频。视频无字幕，意在让学生专注于视听过程，快速反应出It's about a cat.从而引出动画的主角 Mr Black黑猫警长和配角mouse（mice），借助配图的单词卡片帮助学生理解名词变复数的特殊变化。之后提出问题How does the cat feel? How do the mice feel?让学生观看字幕版视频，引出The cat is angry. The mice are afraid of him.并板书核心句型进行教读，同时指导连读。学生在两次视听整体输入中了解对话文本的大意并学习核心句型。借助PPT一句一句的呈现对话文本的内容，引导学生听音模仿。教师根据学生的实时掌握情况有针对性地进行发音、语调和情感指导。教师运用《黑猫警长》的动画片段帮助学生理解模音时出现的难点词汇chases，并引导学生通过现场表演的形式解读难点词汇chasing。以问答互动的形式帮助学生理解 Why is the cat angry with the mice?在对话的操练环节，教师使用了Shadow reading影子跟读、学生示范、小组合作表演等方式，引导学生投入对话表演。之后借助自编歌曲以慢、中、快三种速度，不断复现本课核心词汇和句型，帮助学生突破重点和难点。在拓展环节，教师首先借助图片引导学生回顾、谈论对话主要内容，并尝试填词描述动画片《黑猫警长》的主要内容。然后引导学生运用本课核心句型比较外国动画Tom and Jerry与《黑猫警长》中猫鼠角色的异同。最后引导学生运用核心词句尝试描述自己最喜欢的卡通片，将语言运用上升到精神和情感层面。通过各式卡通内容的分享，引导学生体会不同的动画片带给我们的多样感受。

案例视频

（济南市经五路小学
王　冠）

五、课后训练

根据PEP《英语(三年级起点)》六年级上册 Unit 4 I have a pen pal 中的 Let's talk 部分，撰写一份教学设计并试讲。

语音教学

◆ 了解语音教学的功能
◆ 识别语音教学的内容
◆ 运用常用教学方法组织教学
◆ 教学设计中能够运用自然拼读教学法

一、语音教学概述

语音是英语学习的基础。英国著名的语音学家吉姆森（A. C. Gimson）说过："一个人要想学会任何一门语言，只需要学会这门语言百分之五十到九十的语法，百分之一的词汇就足够了，但是必须百分之百地掌握这门语言的语音知识。"语音教学承担着重要的语音基础性任务，是语言教学的重要内容之一。自然规范的语音和语调，将为有效的口语交际奠定良好的基础。语音教学应注重语义与语境、语调与语流相结合，通过大量听音、模仿和实践，引导学生发现读音规律。将语音教学与单元话题和情景相融合，引导学生在感知理解语言的基础上，体会语音的表意功能，帮助学生形成语音意识和拼读能力，促进学生正确发音习惯的形成，为准确、得体地表达与交流奠定基础。在语言使用中，语法知识是形式的统一体，与语音、词汇、语篇和语音知识相连，直接影响语言理解与表达的准确性和得体性。

目前被广泛使用的不同版本的小学英语教材都对语音教学有所涉及。如PEP《英语（三年

级起点）》（人民教育出版社）中的Let's spell部分，《英语（牛津上海版）》（上海教育出版社）中的Learn the sounds部分，新标准英语（外研社版）中的Listen and repeat部分，都是专门针对语音进行学习的板块。以PEP《英语（三年级起点）》（人民教育出版社）四年级上册中的Unit 3 Let's spell部分为例，引导学生观察总结nose, note, coke和Mr Jones，发现字母o在开音节和闭音节中的发音区别，启发学生自主发现语音规律。

二、常用教学方法与活动

1. 利用歌曲与歌谣

案例一

活动名称：Let's chant

活动意图：以歌谣的形式练习字母在单词中的发音，朗朗上口，好记有趣。

活动内容：教师领读歌谣，配以节奏，学生诵读。

歌曲歌谣应用于语音教学，通过由词成句，由句成篇的歌谣，将拼读规律融合其中，学生们在趣味吟诵和歌唱中，自主发现规律，有助于自主学习能力的提升。以PEP《英语（三年级起点）》五年级上册Unit 6 In a nature park中的Let's spell部分为例。例词"house, mouse, sound, count"呈现了字母组合ou的发音规律。教师可以利用例词创编歌谣，并配上节奏，教给学生们吟诵。例如：

Sh! Sh! What's that sound?

A little mouse is on the ground.

A little mouse is in my house.

I can't count!

Sh! Sh! Sh! Sh!

这个歌谣呈现了一幅栩栩如生的画面：屋里突然有动静，小声一点，看到了一只老鼠，又一只老鼠，数不清有几只老鼠……歌谣朗朗上口，易学好记，创设了生动的画面，又将语音规律巧妙地包含其中。在实际教学中，教师可以先呈现歌谣，带领学生吟诵，然后启发学生自主找出例词，发现拼读规律，促进学生自主探究能力的提升。

2. 使用自然拼读教具

案例二

活动名称： Let's spell

活动意图： 利用拼读闪卡，拼读翻翻台历练习发音，启发学生自主找到拼读规律。

活动内容： 教师利用拼读闪卡，翻翻台历，带领学生练习拼读，培养拼读意识。

小学语音教学应充分利用丰富的教学工具。闪卡，翻翻台历等都是在日常教学中常用的教学工具。教具色彩艳丽，变化丰富，玩法简单，一方面增加了课堂教学的趣味性，将枯燥乏味的拼读练习变成有趣的游戏竞赛，另一方面增加了学生的参与性，可以整班活动，小组活动，单人活动，丰富了课堂活动的组织形式。

以《新标准英语（一年级起点）》（外研版）五年级下册Module 2 Unit 2中的Listen and say部分为例：制作闪卡aw, air, ass, dr, s, h, ch, cl, p，固定闪卡aw，分别用闪卡dr, s进行替换拼读练习；固定闪卡air，分别用闪卡ch, h进行替换拼读练习；固定闪卡ass，分别用闪卡cl, p进行替换拼读练习。以小组活动形式开展，并进行课堂展示。随后启发同学们思考，还有哪些单词包含aw,哪些单词包含air,还可以打破课本所给例词的限制,用手里的闪卡拼出新的单词,并完成拼读。

4 Listen and say. 🎧

aw	air	ass
draw	chair	class
saw	hair	pass

3. 利用绘本故事

案例三

活动名称:Let's read

活动意图:利用绘本故事拓展练习拼读规律。

活动内容:教师讲解拼读规律,学生练习例词及故事,巩固字母在单词中的发音。

教师在教学过程中,可以有针对性地选择绘本,拓展教学内容。在绘本教学中,我们要将语音教学与故事教学相结合,为学生提供足够的语言学习支架,包括拼读规律,视觉词的学习等,降低绘本学习的难度,将语音教学与语境、语义结合,把语音学习变成一件有意思的学习活动。

以《丽声拼读故事会》一级第三课Bob Bug为例:故事讲了小虫子Bob一家人的生活,图文并茂,生动有趣,为语音学习提供了语境和语义。教师可以带领学生在图片的帮助下,理解故事大意,然后找出故事中有相同发音规则的词,通过跟读仿读,启发学生发现语音规律。例如,故事中出现了bad,dad两个词,教师可以启发学生发现字母a在闭音节中的发音。教师可以利用故事中的mum、bug、cup、hug,启发学生发现字母u在闭音节中的发音,利用故事中的get、leg来总结字母e在闭音节中的发音,故事中还有fit、lid、sit来复习字母i在闭音节中的发音。故事将元音字母a, e, i, o, u在闭音节中的发音进行了综合利用并赋予有趣的情节。利用绘本故事讲解语音,让学生们在学习的过程中读懂故事,理解语境和语义,同时综合运用拼读规则朗读故事,真正实现了"语义与语境,语调与语流统一结合"的教学理念。

三、教学片段模拟训练

片段一

PEP《英语（三年级起点）》三年级下册 Unit 6 How many? 中的 Let's spell

Presentation（新授环节）

T: Hello, boys and girls. Look at the pictures on the blackboard. Can you tell me what are they?

Ss: Hand, dog, leg, duck, big.

T: Excellent!

T: Now look at the red letter in each word. What do "a, e, i, o, u" say?

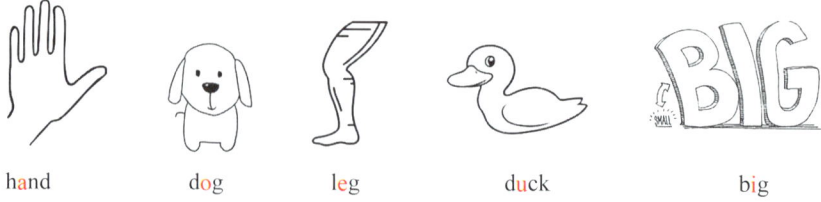

hand   dog   leg   duck   big

Ss: A, e, i, o, u.

T: Great job! Let's fill in the blanks and chant together.

T &Ss: *My hand has five little fingers.*

My legs have ten little toes.

My dog has one cute little face.

But my duck has one big nose.

T:　Great job! Now I have another chant for you. After chanting, please tell me what words have the sound of " a, e, i, o, u ".

I can see a ...

I can see a rat.

The rat is behind the cap.

I can see a hen.

The hen is near the desk.

I can see a fish.

The fish is in the river.

I can see a dog.

The dog is on the log.

I can see a duck.

The duck is under the umbrella.

How funny!

【设计意图】课本上歌谣的四个分句呈现了元音字母a,e,i, o,u 在闭音节中的发音规律。教师可以结合简笔画、动作、拟声呈现hand, leg, dog, duck, big这五个包含发音规律的例词,使学生在诵读的过程中将词的音、形、义相结合,激发学生们的思维,使其在图片、声音的帮助下立体直观地习得语音知识。教师还可以根据发音规律创编新的歌谣进行巩固练习,鼓励学生自主发现拼读规律,促进其辩证思维能力的形成。

案例视频

（练习者：张爽爽）

片段二

PEP《英语(三年级起点)》三年级下册Unit 4 Where is my car? 中的Let's spell。

Practice（巩固拓展环节）

T:　We have learned "dog, box, orange, body" , and o says /ɒ/. Now let's play a spelling game. I will choose one student from Team A and one from Team B. Listen carefully and use the flash cards to spell the words that you hear. Let's begin!

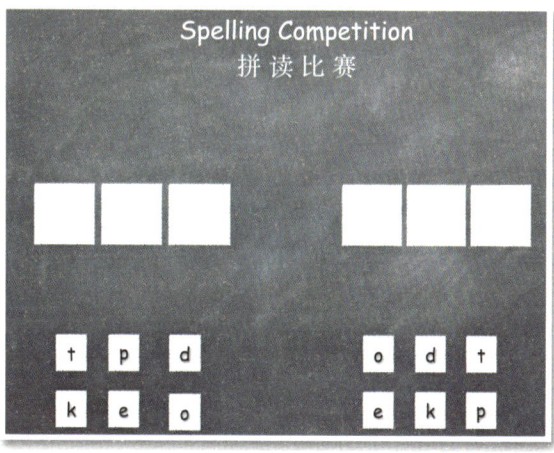

T: T-O-P TOP; D-O-T DOT.

Ss use the flashcards to spell the words "top" and "dot".

T: Excellent! Another game for you. It is called "Shooting Game". Let your hands be your gun and shoot and say the word you see. Let's begin!

T: Now I will introduce a new book for you.（出示《攀登英语阅读系列——有趣的字母》）After reading this story, please tell me what "o" words you can find.

Ss read the story and find the "o" words: fox, dog, clock, frog, and doll.

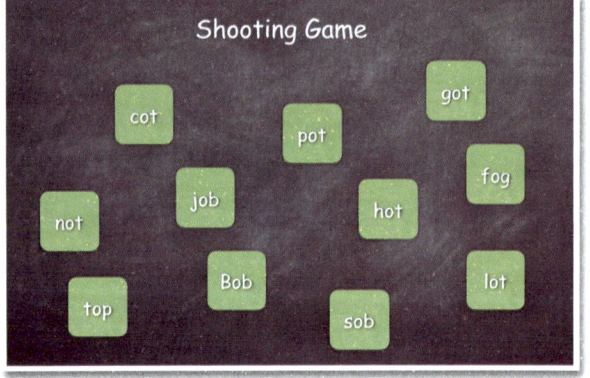

【设计意图】本课例重点学习元音字母o在闭音节中的发音。通过本节课的学习，学生能够正确读出闭音节中o的发音，并根据拼读规律，拼读coc结构的单词的读音。本片段为练习环节，主要包含分组闪卡拼读练习、拼读比赛等环节。多样丰富的练习模式，将枯燥的语音训练变得生动有趣，有效巩固了新知，又进行了拓展。英文绘本阅读环节综合所学知识，以故事的形式巩固拓展拼读规律，培养学生的发散思维能力。

案例视频

（练习者：吕芳雅）

四、范例导读

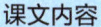

课 文 来 源

PEP《英语（三年级起点）》三年级下册 Unit 3 At the zoo

单元整体设计

（一）教材内容

课文内容

（二）单元教学内容与要求

主题模块	学 习 内 容			学习水平	学习与评价要求
1 语音	1.1　读音规则	1.1.1　闭音节中字母i的发音规律		A	知晓闭音节的特征，及字母i在闭音节中的发音
2 词汇	2.1　核心词汇：thin，fat，tall，short，long，small，big			C	背记、理解与运用thin，fat，tall，short，long，small，big
3 词法	3.1　名词	3.1.1　可数名词单复数与be动词的搭配		A	知晓可数名词单复数与be动词的搭配
	3.2　形容词	3.2.1　形容词		A	知晓形容词在句中描述事物特征的功能
	3.3　动词	3.3.1　be动词		A	知晓be动词必须与主语的单复数搭配的用法
4 句法	4.1　句子种类	4.1.1　陈述句		C	用陈述句It's .../It has ...简单描述动物的特征
		4.1.2　祈使句		C	用祈使句来发出指令
5 语篇	5.1　记叙文	5.1.1　基本信息	Start to read	B	用简单的句型描述事物特征
			Story time	A	通过动物的特征判断动物种类，并发现不同

备注：A 知晓　B 理解　C 运用

（三）单元教学与评价目标

1. 语言运用目标

学生能在动物园的语境中，借助图片和文字，运用核心词汇thin，fat，tall，short，long，small，big等及核心句型It's .../It has ...简单描述动物的特征。按照正确的意群及语音、语调朗读文本。

2. 知识技能目标

（1）学生能知晓英语字母i在闭音节中的发音。

（2）学生能在语境中知晓、理解、背记并运用核心词汇thin，fat，tall，short，long，small，big简单表达动物的特征。

（3）学生能在语境中理解并运用核心句型It's .../It has ...描述介绍动物。

（4）学生能在语境中听懂、读懂语篇并提取相关信息，能够按照正确的意群及语音、语调朗读故事，并运用本单元所学核心句型描述动物，同时能够根据阅读所获信息完成配对连线。

（5）学生能通过看图捕捉主要信息，并根据提示做出听前预测；能够通读文段，获取主旨大意和细节信息，并能进行推理判断。

3. 语言情感目标

学生能够热爱大自然，爱护动物。

（四）分课时教学与评价目标

课时与板块	知识与技能	语用与情感	评价活动
第一课时 P24 Let's talk Draw and say	1. 能读懂题目要求，在听前预测听力重点，能运用听力技巧完成听力任务 2. 能理解、朗读并背记核心词汇short，tall，fat 3. 能感知、理解、正确运用核心句型Look at .../It's ...描述动物的特征 4. 能在语境中感知、理解对话内容并能模仿读演对话	能在语境中借助图文模仿读演对话，做到语言基本正确，表达比较流利并且有一定情感	1. 能理解、朗读并背记核心词汇short，tall，fat 2. 能正确运用核心句型Look at .../It's ...描述动物的特征
第二课时 P25 Let's learn Let's do	1. 能理解、朗读核心词汇fat，thin，tall，short 2. 能在语境下正确使用Look at .../It's ...描述动物的特征	在介绍动物语境中，运用核心语言描述动物的特征，语音语调准确、内容完整达意、表达流利	根据动作提示的情境，准确、连贯地表达特征
第三课时 P26 Let's spell	能在教师的启发下，发现元音i在闭音节中的发音规律，并正确朗读	发现规律总结规律	根据图片提示及发音规律书写单词
第四课时 P27-P28 Let's talk Let's learn Let's do	1. 读懂题目要求，在听前预测听力重点，能运用听力技巧完成听力任务 2. 理解、朗读并背记核心词汇small，big，short，long	1. 在语境中借助图文模仿读演对话，做到语言基本正确，表达比较流利并且有一定情感	根据提示对应图片，并根据设定的语境，展演对话

（续表）

课时与板块	知识与技能	语用与情感	评价活动
第四课时 P27~P28 Let's talk Let's learn Let's do	3. 用It has …描述动物的特征 4. 在语境中感知、理解对话内容并能模仿读演对话	2. 养成热爱动物保护动物的好品质	
第五课时 P29 start to read	1. 读懂描述动物特征的句子,完成图片与文字的连线 2. 综合运用本单元的核心词句来完整表达核心话题的任务	描述动物特征	完成描述动物特征的任务
第六课时 P30~P31 Let's check Let's sing Story time	1. 通过阅读趣味故事,复习巩固动物的名称,增加语言的输入 2. 正确完成听力练习 3. 通过阅读获得有效信息,并完成与图片的对应	体会到情感的变化对故事情节的推动作用	小组合作表演故事根据图片和文字提示与小组成员分享即时心情

课时教学设计

PEP《英语（三年级起点）》三年级下册 Unit 3 At the zoo 第三课时 Let's spell

【设 计 者】济南市市中区育秀小学　周淑娟

【教学流程】

I. Warm-up	II. Presentation and practice	III. Consolidation and extension	IV. Homework
Greeting Sing a song Revise the sounds of letters	Present the sound of /ɪ/ Chant with the video Make and blend the words	Learn to read (1) Learn to read (2)	Blend more words Read the stories Retell the story

【教学设计】

一、教学目标

知识目标:

1. 学生能够掌握元音字母i的短音音素,把握好嘴型特征。

2. 学生能够拼读并且理解以下词汇,如: big,pig,six,milk,gift,six 等。

3. 学生能够尝试拼读歌谣,在感知地道读音的基础上,修正自己的朗读。

能力目标：

1.学生能够养成主动拼读单词的过程，即：先主动说出每个字母的音素；然后将音素组合，并形成一个完整读音的过程。

2.学生能够在对比自己读音和磁带读音的基础上，有意识地修正自己的朗读。

3.学生能够运用 i 的拼读规律，认读单词并根据配图理解小故事。

情感、文化、学习策略：

通过拼读的方式，让学生体会单词读音形成的过程，激发学生对英语学习的热情和信心，进而形成自主拼读的意识，掌握获取单词读音的方法。

二、教学重难点

1.重点

元音字母 i 的嘴型和发音；学生拼读单词的过程。

2.难点

如何在拼读出单词读音之后，有效提升语音水准，比如语调、节奏以及最后一个辅音的处理等。

三、教具准备

实物、活动用纸、短语卡片、PPT

四、教学过程

Teaching steps	Teacher's Activities	Ss' activities
I. Warm-up	1. Sing and act. T: Hello, boys and girls! How are you? T: Before our class, let's sing a song about letters and try to do the actions. T: Now sing and act with me. 2. Revise the sounds of letters. Quick answer T: You will see some letters. Please say the sounds that the letters make.	Ss: Hello, Olivia. Ss sing with the teacher. A is for apple, /æ/, /æ/, apple. B is for bag, /b/,/b/,bag. ... Ss: Yes. S1: l makes /l/ S2: i makes /ɪ/ S3: t makes /t/ S4: f makes /f/
II. Presentation and practice	1. Present the sound of /ɪ/ T: There is a word puzzle for you. Can you guess who he is? A riddle (猜谜语) I'm an animal. I'm big. *big* I'm pink. I like to eat . I like to sleep. What am I ? pig *pig*	S1: It is a pig. Ss read the puzzle. Ss chant. *I see a pig.* *The pig is big.* *The pig is pink.* *I see a pig.* *A big pink pig.*

（续表）

Teaching steps	Teacher's Activities	Ss' activities
II. Presentation and practice	T: Please try to read the puzzle. **Let's chant** I see a ___pig___. The pig is ___big___. The pig is ___pink___. A big pink ___pig___. I see a ___pig___. A big pink ___pig___. T: Look at these words. They all have "i" in the words. What sound does "i" make? pin　kid　fin wig　dig hit 2. Chant. 　T: Let's watch a video and see what does the pig like to do. 3. Make and blend the words. 　T: Can you make more words? 　Take out your letters and try to make more words. 4. Make and spell. 　T: Listen to me. I read the words and you try to spell the words on your desk.	S2: It sounds /ɪ/. The pig likes to dig. Ss chant along the video. Ss make new words and read them. Ss listen carefully. S1: lit　S2: wit　S3: rib (on the blackboard)
III. Consolidation and extension	**Learn to read (1)** 1. Share a story with the student. 　T: My friend pig and his friend cat go to park to pick up the garbage. (teacher acts to help students understand) Look, the pig has a ...? 　What about the cat? 　T: Can you say the sentence? ... 　Teacher shows the cards. 2. Teacher guides the students to read this story. 3. Make the story a chant.	S1: bag, b-a-g, bag S2 : bin, b-i-n, bin S3: The cat has a bin. S4: A lid and a rag. S5: A tag and a tin can. Ss read the story. Ss chant the story. *Pig has a bag.* *Cat has a bin.* *What can go in the bag?* *A lid and a rag.* *What can go in the bin?* *A tag and a tin can.*

（续表）

Teaching steps	Teacher's Activities	Ss' activities
III. Consolidation and extension	LET'S CHANT Pig has a bag. Cat has a bin. What can go in the bag? A lid and a rag. What can go in the bin? A tag and a tin can. **Learn to read (2)** 1. Play a game. Try to open the gift and guess what's in the box. sit if is pig milk dish thin 2. Teacher tells a story about Jack and Mick. T: Can you read the name of the story? What's this? It's a raft. Who has a big raft? Can you read this sentence? What does Mick have? What happen then? 3. Read and act. T: Read the story in groups and try to act. Jack and Mick Jack has a bid raft. Mick has a big pack. The raft dips and tips. Jack and Mick dip and tip. Mick kicks the pack! Will the pack sink? Will Mick get it back? Mick picks it up! Tips: 1.自读小故事，请根据今天所学的字母i的拼读规律朗读故事。2.遇到不会的单词结合图片和上下文大胆猜测，有困难请举手问老师。 4. Show time.	Ss read the words on the PPT. Ss read the name of the story. S1: Jack has a raft. S2: Mick has a big pack. Ss read the story by themselves and then read in groups. Ss read and act in groups. Ss show their stories.

（续表）

Teaching steps	Teacher's Activities	Ss' activities
IV. Homework	1. Blend more words 2. Read the stories 3. Retell the story	
Blackboard design		

【设计思路】

本课围绕语音教学开展了语音、书写和阅读三部分逐步递进的教学活动。语音部分主要学习字母 i 在单词中的短音发音 /ɪ/。通过拆音、拼音和分类等活动，以谜语、歌谣的形式展开，培养学生的语音意识，帮助学生自主归纳字母 i 在单词中的短音发音 /ɪ/，促进学生归纳总结思维能力的培养。书写部分训练，以描红单词活动实现，培养学生初步掌握单词书写和辨认词形的能力，完成从听到写的转化。最后，教师通过两个配图小故事，培养学生运用 i 拼读规律认读单词和根据配图理解故事的能力，对拼读规律的学习进行了巩固和拓展。

案例视频

（济南市市中区育秀小学 周淑娟）

五、课后训练

根据 PEP《英语（三年级起点）》五年级上册 Unit 3 What would you like? 中的 Let's spell 部分，撰写一份教学设计并试讲。

学习目标

◆ 了解读写教学的功能
◆ 识别读写教学的内容
◆ 运用常用教学方法组织教学
◆ 教学设计能够结合多学科知识并注重读写策略的渗透

一、读写教学概述

阅读和写作是语言教学的一体两面,两者既相对独立又密切联系。阅读是语言的输入,可以帮助学生积累词汇,掌握句法,学习遣词造句、布局谋篇的写作技巧,为语言的输出做好准备。同时,阅读对儿童的认知能力、语言能力和社会发展能力的提升,情感态度的形成都有积极的影响。写作则是语言的输出,把想法转变成文字,通过文字传递信息,表达思想情感态度。阅读与写作密不可分,小学英语教学通常将这两个部分密切结合,共同教学。

小学英语读写教学要着重培养学生读和写的学习能力。其中看图识词,在指认物体的前提下认读所学词语,读懂教材中简短的要求或指令,能借助图片读懂简单的故事或小短文并养成按意群阅读的习惯,正确朗读所学故事或短文,掌握一定的阅读策略,培养自主分析问题解决问题的独立思考能力,发展语言应用能力和思维能力,都是英语学科核心素养在阅读教学中的体现。就写作教学而言,其目标是教会学生正确书写字母和单词,在有意义的语境中抄写单词、仿写句子,根据文章中提供的信息补全文本、仿写描述性小短文,培养创新精神和逻辑思维。写作教学要真正培养学生用英语解决问题的能力。

目前各个版本的教材都对读写教学进行了编排。如PEP《英语(三年级起点)》(人民教育出版社)中的 Read and write 部分,《英语(牛津上海版)》(上海教育出版社)中的 Look and read, Ask and answer 等部分,《英语(三年级起点)》(外语教学与研究出版社)中 Write, read and do 部分,都是专门针对读写进行学习的板块。以PEP《英语(三年级起点)》六年级上册 Unit 2 Ways to go to school 中的 Read and write 部分为例,内容为不同国家的孩子们上学的不同方式。

小学英语读写教学对学生英语学科核心素养的提升有重大影响,对他们的人生观、价值观和世界观的形成也有深远影响。教师应选择合适的阅读内容,多样的文体形式,在教学中将英语学科知识与相关学科的知识融为一体,关注儿童的阅读体验与感悟思辨,引导学生掌握多种阅读策略,提高快速获取文本信息的能力,并将掌握的文本信息根据一定的写作步骤转变成文字,使学生在读写方法、习惯、兴趣等方面打下扎实基础。

二、常用教学方法与活动

(一)阅读教学常用活动与策略
1. 读前、读中、读后三段式阅读教学

案例

> **活动名称:**Pre-reading,While-reading and Post-reading
>
> **活动意图:**在不同阶段采取丰富多样的活动,引导学生更加深入有效地阅读。
>
> **活动内容:**阅读教学分为读前、读中和读后三个部分,在不同阶段开展不同教学活动。

(1)读前活动。

读前活动是指开始阅读前的教学活动。读前活动目的是帮助学生建立知识联系,激活已有认知,感知文段中的相关语言表达,为开始阅读做好准备。常用的读前活动与策略包括:

① 头脑风暴。

教师提出主题,围绕这个主题启发学生进行联想和讨论活动,激活学生的已有认知体系,建立知识之间的联系。例如PEP《英语(三年级起点)》五年级上册Unit 3 What would you like?的单元主题为食物,教师可以在读前活动中提出围绕食物进行头脑风暴活动。

② 梳理已有知识,预测文本内容。

基于学生已有知识或者头脑风暴活动的讨论结果,启发学生预测阅读文本的内容。教师可以采用思维导图、简笔画、挂图等板书形式,将对阅读文本内容的预测进行梳理。

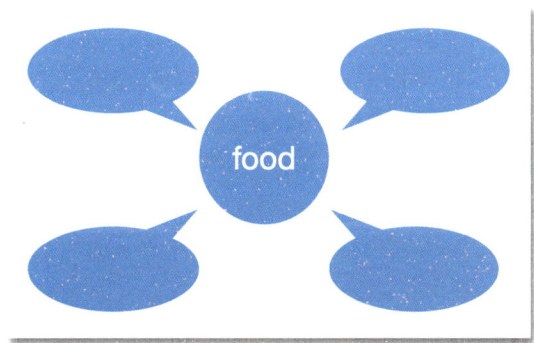

③ 读前设问。

读前设问活动可由教师启发学生完成，利用KWL图表，带着问题与预测进行阅读。以问题为引导深入感知，为阅读活动做准备。

④ 小组讨论。

学生将语篇的主题、概念、核心语言、文本等与自身经历和体验相联系，开展小组讨论，记录整理并分享。

⑤ 视觉辅助。

教师提供与主题相关的图片、简笔画、PPT、视频等辅助教学，有助于调动学生多种感官反应，激发学生学习兴趣，帮助学生建立知识联系，提升学科综合能力。

⑥ 扩展阅读。

教师为学生提供与主题语篇相关的扩展阅读资料，帮助学生感知相关语言表达，促进发散思维能力培养。

（2）读中活动。

读中活动是指阅读过程中教师开展的教学活动。读中活动的目的是帮助学生检测读前预测，深入解读作者意图，深入理解文本信息并将获得的信息进行组织。常用的读中活动与策略包括：

① 找出主旨句。

主旨句阐释了段落或者文章的主要思想。学会定位主旨句是学生应该掌握的基本阅读策略之一。

② 确认读前预测与猜想。

基于原有知识和图片信息等进行的读前预测和猜想，在读中进行确认，可以修正读前活动，是读前活动的延续。

③ 回答表象问题和深层次问题。

就文本里的某个信息点进行提问，确认学生的理解。表象问题是学生能够容易识别出的问题。如，时间、地点、人物等。深层次问题能够引发学生的深入思考，需要学生解读作者意图和隐含意义。如，主旨句。

④ 通过语境，猜测生词的含义。

就文章中的生词启发学生通过语境猜测得出含义。

⑤ 不明白或不确定的地方做标记。

提醒学生在阅读过程中，就不明白或者难点进行标记。这是学生应该掌握的有效的阅读策略。

（3）读后活动。

读后活动是指阅读结束后教师开展的教学活动。读后活动目的是帮助学生将读前、读中活动延伸拓展，有意义地运用阅读收获并进一步实现创造，实现文本内容与思维培养和语言运用的高度融合，为写作训练做好准备。常用的读后活动与策略包括：

① 向同学提问。

学生向小组成员提出若干问题，实现生生评价。

② 讨论分享。

学生就文段中最感兴趣的部分做课堂报告，与同学分享。

③ 开展调查。

学生可以根据阅读内容设计调查，就文中涉及的主题内容、情感态度价值观等，向同学发起调查进行深入探讨，从文本走向真实生活。例如，PEP《英语（三年级起点）》四年级上册 Unit 2 My school bag，教师可以创设情境——你的书桌，两人一组合作描述书桌里有什么。

④ 拓展阅读。

学生可以利用互联网、报纸、电视等媒体寻找关于文章主题的内容并进行分享。

⑤ 续写结尾。

续写故事结尾能够培养学生的发散思维能力和语言组织能力。例如《英语》（外研版）五年级上册 Unit 5 There are only nineteen crayons 中的 Listen, read and act out 部分，教师可以启发学生思考 Amy 和 Sam 是怎样解决了问题，进行小组讨论，可以采取句子接龙的形式，例如，Sam says: _____学生们续写故事结尾。

⑥ 绘制读后思维导图。

通过绘制思维导图，实现自我评价，检测阅读理解。

2. 将阅读内容图形化、结构化的教学活动

活动名称：Mind Map

活动意图：利用视觉化、结构化的辅助手段为读写教学建立支撑。

活动内容：教师引导学生由文本主题出发，梳理结构，完成图表填写。

学生在教师的指导与帮助下，将阅读的文本、结构故事的活动链或应用文体的行文顺序、因果关系，以图表或者思维导图的形式呈现，为其仿写和复述提供支撑，有利于学生逻辑

思维能力和批判思维能力的培养。

思维导图的形式也是多种多样，在阅读教学中常用的思维导图有：流程图（flow map）、气泡图（bubble map）、圆圈图（circle map）和树形图（tree map）。

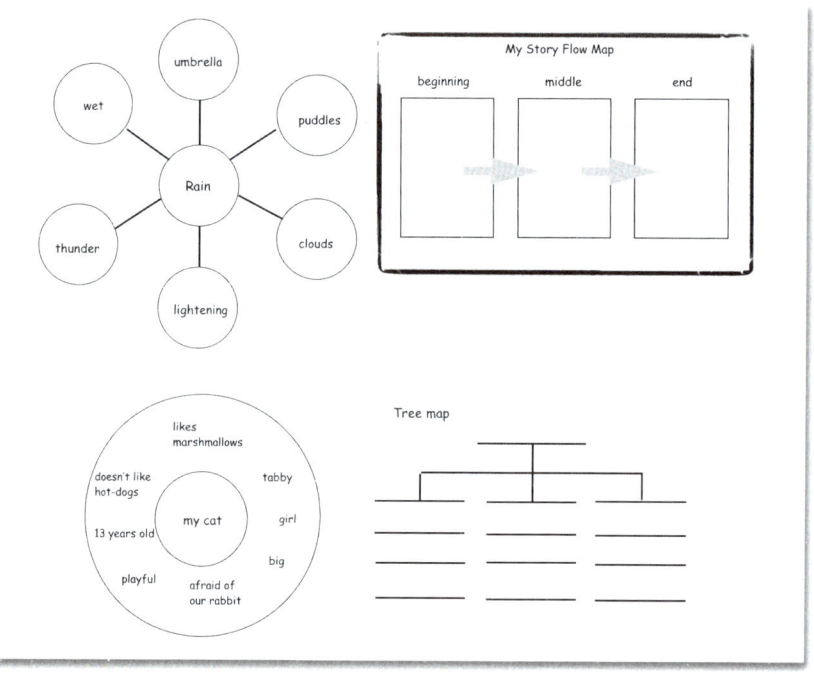

以树形图为例，将其应用于PEP《英语（三年级起点）》五年级下册 Unit 2 My favorite season 中的 Read and write 部分的教学。我们可以绘制树形图，帮助学生梳理文章的脉络。

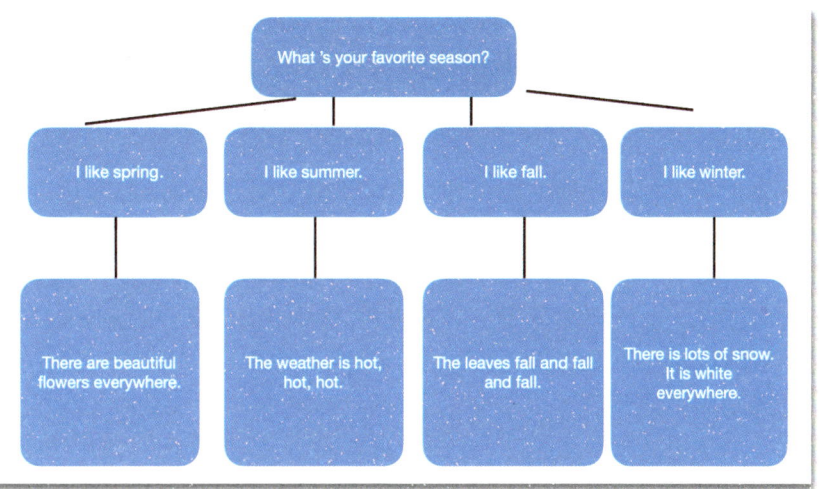

树形图可以帮助学生清晰地梳理出四幅图片中的四个季节和喜欢每个季节的理由,为学生仿写和复述文段打下了基础。

3. 创设多样化的问题情境,帮助学生完成读写

案例

活动名称: Question the text
活动意图: 通过创设多样化的问题情境,让学生带着问题阅读,促进思维能力的培养。
活动内容: 教师提出阶梯性问题,引导学生就文本某个知识点或情感态度等进行回答。

问答式阅读方法是一种有效的阅读教学策略。带着问题进行阅读,可以给学生清晰的阅读目的,将学生的注意力集中在关键内容上,帮助学生在阅读的过程中积极思考,将已知与未知建立联系。问题的设置应体现阶梯性和差异性,在提问与回答练习中,注重学生思维能力的培养。问题的设置有以下五种:

① 单一细节题。

这类问题是对文章中的某一细节进行测试。例如: Who is Robbin? Are these Sarah's blue pants?这类问题的难度低,适用于全体学生,可用于读中、读后,用来评价学生对文章中细节的理解。

② 多元细节题。

这类问题的答案往往出现在文章的多个地方,需要学生思考、搜索并整合答案。例如, What do your family do on Mid-Autumn Day?(PEP《英语》六年级上册 Unit 3 My weekend plan 中的 Read and write 部分)这类问题的难度要大于单一细节题,通过思考与搜索,学生的逻辑思维能力、语言组织能力都可以得到锻炼。多元细节题可用于读中、读后,用来评价学生对文章各个部分的知识点的整合理解。

③ 推测预知题。

这类问题要求学生通过图片、封面、人物、标题等已知的直观信息进行预测,根据已有

知识和经验回答问题。例如，What can you see in this picture? If you were Wu Binbin, what will you do?这类问题的难度适中，问题的创设可根据学生的认知水平，体现差异教学，可用于读前、读中、读后，用来引发学生的思考，锻炼其逻辑推理能力。

④ 情感态度题。

这类问题要求学生根据先前的知识和经验并结合文章组织语言，表达自己的情感。例如，What's your opinion about the modern transportation?这类问题的难度较大，教师在创设问题时，应建立足够的语言支架与知识支架，让学生可以用已经掌握的词汇和句型，准确地表达个人的感受与态度。这类问题可用于读前猜测，读中评论，读后情感升华，对学生的思维品质和文化品格的培养有积极的意义。

⑤ 主旨提炼题。

这类问题要求学生利用阅读策略，全面理解整篇语义，准确地总结出文章的主旨大意。例如，What does this passage mainly talk about?这类问题的难度较大，教师在创设问题前，应指导学生使用适当的阅读策略进行分段式阅读。这类问题可用于读后总结，有利于学生学习能力和思维品质的培养。

（二）写作教学常用方法与活动

学生开始参与写作到学会写作是一个漫长的过程。写作练习应该从易到难，从词到句，从句到篇，逐步推进。

1. 仿写

案例

活动名称： Imitative Writing

活动意图： 利用阅读获得核心句型，启发学生发现规律，为写作建立支撑。

活动内容： 教师引导学生按照题目的提示，完成仿照练习。

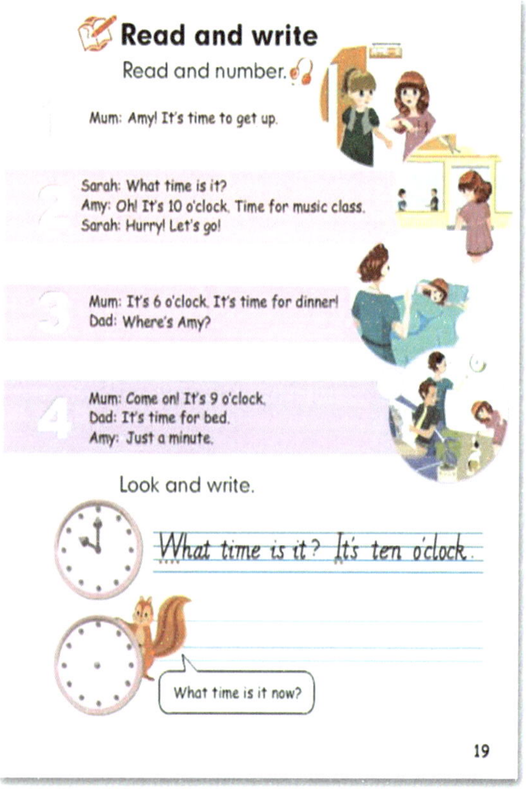

通过阅读获得的信息，按照题目的提示，完成仿照练习，是学习写作的第一步。以PEP《英语》四年级下册Unit 2 What time is it?中的Read and write部分为例。

本单元的核心句型为What time is it? It's ... o'clock. 教师引导学生找出核心句型，并自行在小松鼠的钟表上画出时针分针，让学生仿照上句写出句子。

2. 补全信息

补全信息练习预留出的填空处，往往

是文段信息的核心内容。从填写文段的主要信息入手,组成完整的句式,进而组织成一段话,为段落写作打下基础。以PEP《英语(三年级起点)》五年级上册 Unit 3 What would you like?中的Read and write部分为例。

> **What would you like to eat? Write to Robin, please.**
>
> Dear Robin,
>
> My favourite food is _____. It is _____.
>
> I don't like _____ but I like _____.
>
> Thank you!
>
> _____
>
> 29

学生可以根据自己的饮食喜好,填写自己喜欢的食物和不喜欢的食物,补全信息形成段落,为段落写作打好基础。

三、教学片段模拟训练

片段一

PEP《英语(三年级起点)》四年级上册 Unit 2 My school bag中的 Read and write

Warm-up(启动环节)

1. Brain storming

T: Look, this is Lilei's schoolbag. Let's guess what is in it.

S: A Math book, a ruler, a story book, an English book ...

【设计意图】读前活动中开展头脑风暴活动,启发学生根据常识和之前学过的知识猜测书包里有什么,学生的思维和已有的知识经验被激活。

2. Draw a mind map

T: We just talked about Lilei's schoolbag. Now we are in our classroom, can you find the things in your desk? Please finish this mind map.

【设计意图】读前活动中绘制发散思维导图,帮助学生梳理知识,为口头表达和写作建立语言支架。

Read and write

Read and circle.

What is in your schoolbag?
I have two storybooks, three keys, some candies, some toys and a cute panda in my schoolbag.

A   B

Look, choose and write.
What is in it?

I have three _____, an _____, a _____.
and a _____ in my desk.

bag pen pencil keys notebook candy egg

What's in your desk?

I have _____ in my desk.

19

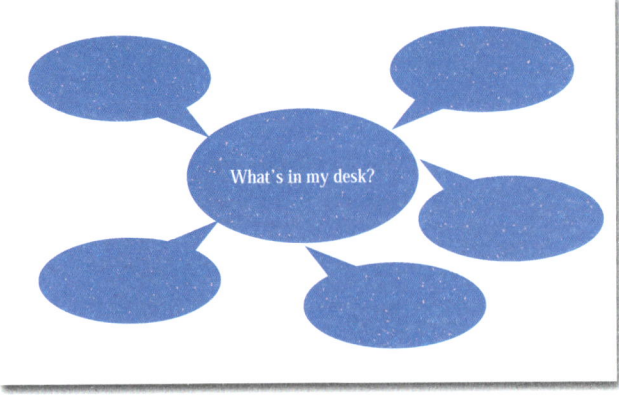

案例视频

（练习者：李媛媛）

片段二

PEP《英语（三年级起点）》五年级上册 Unit 3 What would you like? 中的 Read and write

Practice（练习环节）

1. Pair Work

T: Discuss with your partner about what food Wu Binbin and grandpa like and don't like, then fill in the chart.

【设计意图】练习巩固环节属于读后活动,教师组织学生小组讨论,然后完成思维导图,将文本信息以图表、思维导图的形式呈现,为其复述和仿写提供了支撑,有利于学生逻辑思维能力的培养。

2. Do a survey

T: Ask your friends about what food he/she likes and doesn't like, fill in the chart. Then introduce his/her eating habits according to your chart.

Eating habits

Name	Age	boy/girl	food he/she likes	food he/she doesn't like

【设计意图】创设情境,组织学生对朋友的饮食习惯进行调查,利用所学单词与核心句型进行描述并完成表格。从文本走向生活,启发学生对健康饮食习惯的思考与讨论,真正实现用英语做事情的课程目标。

案例视频

(练习者:曾煜婷)

四、范例导读

课 文 来 源

PEP《英语(三年级起点)》四年级上册 Unit 4 My home

单元整体设计

(一)教材内容

课文内容

(二)单元教学内容与要求

主题模块	学 习 内 容			学习水平	学习与评价要求
1 语音	1.1 读音规则	1.1.1 开音节中字母u的发音规律		A	知晓字母u在开音节中的发音
2 词汇	2.1 核心词汇:bedroom,living room,study,kitchen,bathroom,bed,phone,table,sofa,fridge			C	背记、理解与运用bedroom,living room,study,kitchen,bathroom,bed,phone,table,sofa,fridge
3 词法	3.1 名词	3.1.1 可数名词单复数与be动词的搭配		A	知晓可数名词单复数与be动词的搭配
	3.2 形容词	3.2.1 介词		A	知晓介词在句中表地点的功能
	3.3 动词	3.3.1 be动词		A	知晓be动词必须与主语的单复数搭配的用法
4 句法	4.1 句子种类	4.1.1 陈述句		C	用陈述句He/She is in … They are in …等简单表达人和物品的位置
		4.1.2 疑问句	4.1.2.1 特殊疑问句	C	用特殊疑问句Where is/are …进行提问,并回答It is … They are in … He/She is in …
		4.1.3 祈使句		C	用祈使句来发出指令
5 语篇	5.1 记叙文	5.1.1 基本信息	Read and write	B	说明文基本信息的获得和描述
			Story time	A	简单讲述对话中的时间、地点、人物、事件等基本信息

备注:A 知晓 B 理解 C 运用

（三）单元教学与评价目标

1. 语言运用目标

学生能在my home的语境中，借助图片和文字，运用核心词汇bedroom, living room, study, kitchen, bathroom, bed, phone, table, sofa, fridge 等及核心句型 Where is/are ..., It is ..., They are in ..., He/she is in ... 简单表达房间的陈设及人的位置。按照正确的意群及语音、语调朗读文本。

2. 知识技能目标

（1）学生能知晓英语字母u在开音节中的发音。

（2）学生能在语境中知晓、理解、背记并运用核心词汇bedroom, living room, study, kitchen, bathroom, bed, phone, table, sofa, fridge, 简单表达房间的陈设及人的位置。

（3）学生能在语境中理解并运用核心句型 Where is/are ...?It is ..., They are in ... He/she is in ...描述任何物品的位置，介绍自己的房间。

（4）学生能在语境中听懂、读懂语篇并提取相关信息；能够按照正确的意群及语音、语调朗读故事，并运用本单元所学核心句型描述房间；能够根据阅读所获信息完成填空并描述位置。

（5）学生能通过看图捕捉主要信息，并根据提示做出听前预测；能够通读文段，获取主旨大意和细节信息，并能进行推理判断。

3. 语言情感目标

学生在家能够做力所能及的家务，学会收拾屋子、把物品摆放整齐，养成良好的生活习惯。

（四）分课时教学与评价目标

课时与板块	知识与技能	语用与情感	评价活动
第一课时 P38 Let's talk Let's play	1. 能读懂题目要求，在听前预测听力重点，能运用听力技巧完成听力任务 2. 能理解、朗读并背记核心词汇living room, study, kitchen 3. 能感知、理解、正确运用核心句型Where is...? Is she in the...? 询问位置，运用She/It is in... 表达人或物体的位置 4. 能在语境中感知、理解对话内容并能模仿读演对话	能在语境中借助图文模仿读演对话，做到语言基本正确，表达比较流利并且有一定情感	完成图片与文字的连线和找寻钥匙位置的任务
第二课时 P39 Let's learn Let's do	1. 能理解、朗读核心词汇bedroom, study, kitchen, living room, bathroom 2. 能在语境下正确使用Where is ...询问地点，并听懂位置的指令	在介绍物体位置的语境中，运用核心语言，询问物体的方位，语音语调准确、内容完整达意、表达流利	根据图片提示的情境，准确、连贯地表达物体的位置
第三课时 P40 Let's spell	能在教师的启发下，发现元音u在开音节中的发音规律，并正确朗读	发现规律、总结规律	根据图片提示及发音规律书写单词

（续表）

课时与板块	知识与技能	语用与情感	评价活动
第四课时 P41 Let's talk Ask, answer and write	1. 能读懂题目要求，在听前预测听力重点，能运用听力技巧完成听力任务 2. 能理解、朗读并背记核心词汇table, phone 3. 能用Where are .../They are ...询问复数名词物品的位置 4. 能在语境中感知、理解对话内容并能模仿读演对话	1. 能在语境中借助图文模仿读演对话，做到语言基本正确，表达比较流利并且有一定情感 2. 养成物品摆放整齐的习惯	根据图片提示给物品找到位置，并根据设定的语境展演对话
第五课时 P42 Let's learn Let's play	1. 能够读懂描述起居室的小文段，完成图片与文字的连线和找寻钥匙位置的任务 2. 能够综合运用本单元的核心词句来完整表达核心话题 3. 能根据例句提示仿写语句，描述自己的房间	能按照顺序描述事物，养成规律生活的习惯	完成按顺序描述自己房间的任务
第六课时 P43–P45 Read and write Let's check Let's sing Story time	1. 能通过阅读趣味故事，复习巩固表达方位的句型My glasses are on ...和询问位置的句型Where are my glasses?增加语言的输入 2. 能正确完成听力练习 3. 能通过阅读获得有效信息，并完成与图片的对应	能体会到情感的变化对故事情节的推动作用	小组合作表演故事，根据图片和文字提示与小组成员分享即时心情

课时教学设计

PEP《英语（三年级起点）》四年级上册 Unit 4 My home 第五课时 Read and write

【设计者】济南市经七路第一小学　刘岩

【教学流程】

I. Warm-up	II. Presentation	III. Practice	VI. Production	V. Homework
Greeting Sing a song Watch and say	listen and choose Let's say Look and say	Look and say Let's chant Let's show Let's give some advice	Group work Show time	Talk about your room and your parents' room. Introduce them to your friends.

【教学设计】

一、教学目标

1. 能够读懂描述起居室的小文段，完成图片与文字的连线和找寻钥匙位置的任务。

2.能够综合运用本单元的核心词句来完整表达核心话题。

3.能够理解阅读文本大意,按照正确的意群及语音、语调朗读文本。

4.能够运用重点句型描述房屋的陈设。

5.通过本课的学习,学生在家能够做力所能及的家务,学会收拾屋子、把物品摆放整齐,养成良好的生活习惯。

二、教学重难点

1.重点

核心句型的具体表达,能够在情景中准确表述物品的位置。

2.难点

综合运用本单元的核心词句来完整表达核心话题。

三、教具准备

PPT、视频、图卡

四、教学过程

Teaching steps	Teachers' activities	Students' activities
I. Warm-up & Lead-in	1. Greeting. 2. Sing a song: On, in, under. 3. Watch and say: Show a big house and the rooms in the house, ask and answer the rooms in the house and the things in the rooms. T: Boys and girls, look, what is it? What rooms do you see in the big house? What do you see in the room?	Students sing the song. Students answer the questions.
II. Presentation	1. Listen and choose. T: Boys and girls, look, who is he? Yes, he is our old friend. He is describing a room. Please listen and choose. "What room is it?" **Listen and choose** (听课文,选择正确的图片。) **What room is it?** (他正在描述什么房间?)	Students listen and choose.

Teaching steps	Teachers' activities	Students' activities
II. Presentation	2. Let's say. T: Wu Binbin is describing his living room. Look at his living room. What do you see in the living room? **Look and say** （看图片，说一说房间的陈设。） What do you see in the living room? I see... 3. Look and say. Teacher shows the pictures of phones and pens. T: Now boys and girls, look, they are also in Binbin's living room. What are they? **Look and say** （看图片，说一说。） 4. Read and find. T: Where are the things? Please read and find. **Read and find** （读课文，找一找这些东西在哪里。）	Students describe the things in the room according to the picture. Answer the names of the things in the room. Students read and find.

（续表）

Teaching steps	Teachers' activities	Students' activities
II. Presentation	T: Where are the books? Where are the pens? Where is the bag? Where are the glasses? 5. Look and say. Look and say. (看图片，说一说。) The _____ is/are _____, and the _____ is/are _____. T: Look at the four pictures. Where are the books and where is the football? He can't find his keys. Can you help him? 6. Reading practice. Listen and read. 1. Intonation 语调 2. Stress 重音 This is my living room. My books are on the sofa, and my pens are on the fridge. My bag is under the table, and my glasses are near the phone. Where are my keys? Can you find them? 7. Read the passage with desk mates. 8. Retell the passage. T: Now, boys and girls, look, these are Wu Binbin's words to describe his room. Can you describe his room in your words? For example: This is my living room. →This is Wu Binbin's living room. Can you finish it like this?	Students read after the tape for two times. 和同桌自读课文一遍 针对原文进行文本的转述，把第一人称转述为第三人称 Students retell the text in pairs.

（续表）

Teaching steps	Teachers' activities	Students' activities
II. Presentation	**Let's describe.** (请用自己的语言描述一下吴彬彬的房间。) This is Wu Binbin's living room. The books are on the sofa, and the pens are on the fridge. The bag is under the table, and the glasses are near the phone. Where are the keys? Can you find them? 	
III. Practice	1. Look and write. **Let's describe.** (请用自己的语言描述一下吴彬彬的房间。) This is_____. _____is/are _____, and_____ is/are_____. _____is/are _____, and_____ is/are_____. Where is/are _____? Can you find it/them? T: Please work in pairs and talk about Wu Binbin's living room. 2. Let's chant. **Let's chant.** This is Wu Binbin's living room. The books are on the sofa, and the pens are on the fridge. The bag is under the table, and the glasses are near the phone. Where are the keys? Can you find them? 3. Let's show. 4. Look, Wu Binbin's room is a little messy. Can you give him some advice? Give some advice to Binbin. (请给Binbin一些整理房间的建议。) Binbin, you can put the_____ in/on/under/near the_____.	Work in pairs and describe Wu Binbin's room and fill in the blanks. All the students do the new chant. Some students show the retelling according to the clues and pictures given on the blackboard. Students give some suggestions to Binbin.

（续表）

Teaching steps	Teachers' activities	Students' activities
IV. Consolidation & Extension	1. Group work. T: Please work in your groups and choose one picture to describe. 2. Show time. 　T: Who'd like to talk about their rooms? 　　Is your room clean? 　　We all like clean rooms. 　　Please keep your rooms clean and tidy. 　　Good habits make all things easy. 	Students choose one picture to describe. Students show the introduction of John and Chen Jie's room.
V. Homework	1. Talk about your rooms and your parents' rooms. 2. Introduce them to your friends.	
Blackboard Design		

【设计思路】

四年级的学生,有了一年英语学习的基础,具备了一定的英语语言能力,英语学习尚处于初级的阶段。他们的模仿力强、求知欲强、记忆力好、表现欲强,但是理解能力较弱。教师利用这一学习特点,围绕教学中的难点、重点设计生动活泼、有趣多样的学习活动,寓教于乐。在教学中重视语音、语调训练,注重模仿、朗读和熟记等实践练习。为了引导学生进行完整语言的表达,提前为学生搭建好语言支架,进行仿说练习,减少了语言输出难度,提高了实效性。

在本课的导入部分,我设计了两个活动。第一个活动是Sing a song。通过一首歌曲,复习本节课需要用到的几个重点方位介词。第二个活动是通过投影的小游戏,对第四单元所学到的有关房屋的名称和房屋里的家具陈设名称进行复习。在呈现第二个活动的时候,我展现出的问题就是What rooms do you see in the house? What do you see in the room?让学生用完整的句子来表达,通过此环节引出本节课的情境。

在呈现练习环节,首先通过Listen and choose活动让学生整体感知文本。由问题What do you see in this room?引导学生认真观察图片,对吴斌斌居室内的物品进行简单描述,强调让学生说完整的句子。之后呈现书本、书包、钢笔和眼镜的图片,进入文本学习,在此过程中教师给出支架The...is/are...,让学生做到完整表述一个句子。在完成找钥匙的任务后,就进入课文的朗读和跟读,练习重点句型的朗读和关键词语的发音。夯实了重难点之后,教师呈现出整篇文本,对吴斌斌的房间进行转述,由表达整句提升到表达整篇。接下来,通过一个chant进行小结。最后的语言输出练习由小组合作完成,旨在锻炼学生语言的综合运用能力。活动设计由浅入深,由句到篇,逐层递进。上课末尾,教师出示干净、整洁的房间图片,引导学生在家能够做力所能及的家务,保持房屋的整洁,总结出 Keep your rooms clean and tidy. Good habits make all things easy.

案例视频

(济南市经七路第一小学
刘　岩)

五、课后训练

根据PEP《英语(三年级起点)》五年级上册Unit 5 There is a big bed 中的 Read and write部分,撰写一份教学设计并试讲。

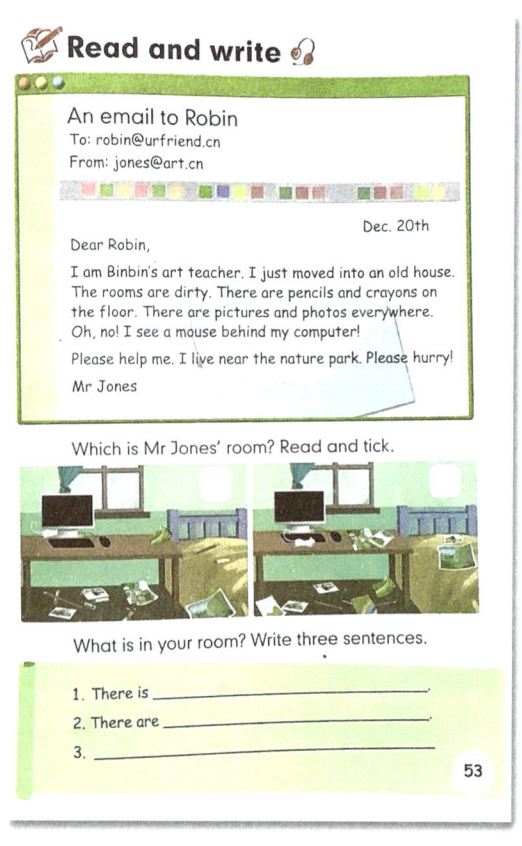

📝 **Read and write** 🎧

An email to Robin
To: robin@urfriend.cn
From: jones@art.cn

Dec. 20th

Dear Robin,

I am Binbin's art teacher. I just moved into an old house. The rooms are dirty. There are pencils and crayons on the floor. There are pictures and photos everywhere. Oh, no! I see a mouse behind my computer!

Please help me. I live near the nature park. Please hurry!

Mr Jones

Which is Mr Jones' room? Read and tick.

What is in your room? Write three sentences.

1. There is _____
2. There are _____
3. _____

53

- 了解故事教学的分类和功能
- 能够选择适合学生的故事
- 能够运用常见教学方法进行故事教学

一、故事教学概述

　　故事教学是以故事为教学资源,以故事的呈现、分析和评价为主要内容的一种教学方式。故事教学的功能除了提高学生语言能力之外,还在于故事所蕴含的教育意义。绘本故事因其图文并茂,寓教于乐,比纯文字的故事更符合小学生的认知特点。原版英文绘本故事语言地道,既有助于学生语言能力的培养,又有利于潜移默化地提升学生的人文素养,是英语教学的好素材。绘本故事题材丰富,如从自然、社会和自我的维度分类,故事 *I am a Bunny* 以小兔子的视角温柔地看待四季的美景,讲述自然界的美好,属于人与自然范畴;*Zoo Day* 描述了小朋友第一次和父母、妹妹参观动物园的场景,属于人与社会范畴;*Giraffes Can't Dance* 讲述了一只不会跳舞的长颈鹿成功逆袭的故事,展示了积极向上的心态,属于自我成长范畴。故事教学既可以在课内也可以在课外开展。

 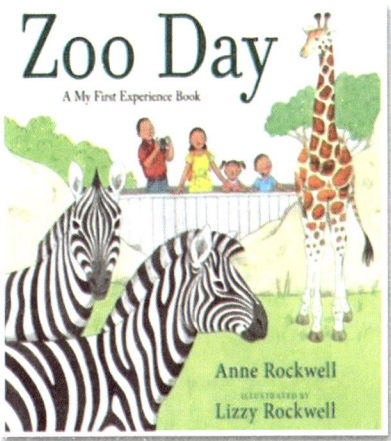 

（一）故事在课内外的运用

1. 故事在课内的运用

目前各个版本的教材精心编排了故事板块内容。如PEP《英语（三年级起点）》中的Story time板块、PEP《英语（新起点）》中的Story time板块、《英语（牛津上海版）》中的Read a story板块、《英语》（译林版）中Cartoon time板块等。以PEP《英语（三年级起点）》六年级上册中的Unit 6 How do you feel?中的Story time为例，具体讲述了Zip等待Zoom做爆米花的故事。通过阅读故事，学生能复习巩固表达感情的句型I'm ...和提出建议的句型 ... should ..., Don't ...，还能了解植物成长的知识。

案例视频

（练习者：刘燕捷）

2. 故事在课外的运用

故事是对课本教学的有益补充。目前，故事在课外的运用大致分为三种情况。

一是利用故事辅助课堂教学。有些故事契合教材的话题或重要知识点，能对教材起到补充、拓展的作用。例如：绘本故事 *I Say, Hello!* 可以作为PEP《英语（三年级起点）》三年级上册第一单元Let's talk的补充材料，用来复习巩固句型I'm ...。

I am a cat. I say, "Meow, meow!" I like milk.

I am a cow. I say, "Moo, moo!" I like grass.

绘本故事 *Wet Legs* 可以作为PEP《英语（三年级起点）》三年级下册第二单元 Let's spell 的课外补充材料,用来巩固字母e在闭音节中的发音 /e/。

A hen.

A pet hen.

A red pet hen.

A red pet hen gets wet.

A red pet hen gets wet and begs.

A red pet hen begs to get in bed.

A red pet hen steps in bed.

WET LEGS!

No red pet hen in bed.

A red pet hen is in the pen.

绘本故事 *The Months of the Year* 可以作为PEP《英语（三年级起点）》五年级下册第三单元Let's learn的补充材料,用来复习巩固12个月份单词及相关节日名称。

January begins the year.
"Happy New Year!"

February is for lovers.
"Will you be my Valentine?"

二是故事阅读与课外活动结合。英语课外活动是课内教学的延伸，是学生英语学习的重要组成部分，能提供给学生更多的语言实践和自主学习的机会。教师可以将故事阅读与课外活动有机结合起来，开展丰富多样、因地制宜的课外活动，如英语朗诵、演唱英语歌曲、讲英语故事、演英语短剧、英语动画配音、英语角、英语演讲会、英语戏剧演出、英语主题班会等，有条件的可以参与社区英语活动、国际学生交流活动等。

三是课后阅读，即不占用课内时间和在校时间，教师推荐一些经典故事书目供学生课后有选择地阅读，以丰富学生的阅读体验、拓展学生自主学习渠道。课后阅读可以结合话题阅读、动画赏析等活动同步开展。例如教师可以推荐给学生 Eric Carle 的故事，开展英语群文阅读。

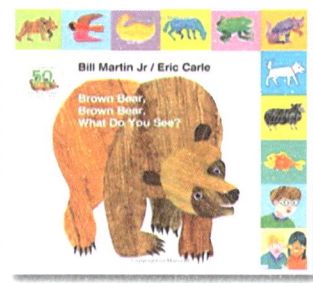

（二）如何选择故事

故事能够提供地道、丰富的语言素材，帮助学生在自然、完整的情境中感受英语的语言魅力和提升人文内涵。选择故事应该从以下几个方面考虑：

1. 故事选择应符合不同年级的阅读目标

不同年级的学生，其阅读目标不尽相同。低年级阅读目标要求以读图为主，辅以说图，旨在让学生感知故事。因此，低年级故事的选择要关注图画的质量，看图画是否表意清晰、精美，是否能吸引小学生的注意力。中年级阅读目标要求读图和说图结合，采用精读猜图的形式开展教学。因此，中年级故事内容要体现逻辑思维能力的锻炼。例如 No David 其中一幅图片描绘大卫在客厅打棒球，妈妈说 Not in the house, David! 接下来的图片中大卫在墙角面壁思过,妈妈说 I said no, David! 这两幅图之间有什么关联? 中间发生了什么? 大卫为什么受罚? 学生需要观察图片、寻找线索,进行推理,找出文字背后的答案。原来是大卫非要在客厅打棒球,结果打碎了花瓶。看,地上破碎的花瓶和角落里的球就是证据。学生就像福尔摩斯一样在图中寻找线索,充满了成就感。

高年级阅读目标要求读、写、创编相结合,既提升读写能力,又拓展学生思维。因此,高年级故事内容要选择适合学生进行创编的绘本。比如绘本 The Hug 中,教师提问 Can you give little Pins a hug? And how? 让学生发散思维,寻找给刺猬一个拥抱的解决方案。

2. 故事选择应贴合教材内容

教学需要是选择故事的前提,故事的选择应贴合教材,体现"教材+"的理念。可以基于同一话题、同一语法现象或同一语音现象选择一篇或几篇英语故事。例如学习完PEP《英语(三年级起点)》四年级上册第二单元Let's spell板块后,教师可以提供给学生以下三个有关"i-e"发音的故事开展英语群文阅读。

3. 故事选择应契合学生的心智发展特点

学生的心智发展既包含学生心理健康发展,也包含记忆、思维、认知等智力发展因素。心智发展随着年龄的增长和教育的增加而呈现出不同的特点。因此,在进行故事选择时,无论从题材、情节还是篇幅上,都应契合学生心智发展特点,适应不同阶段学生的心理和认知发展水平。

（1）故事的题材。

小学生的一个重要特征是好奇。因此，故事的题材应贴近学生生活，富有趣味性和多样性，能激起学生的好奇心和求知欲，让孩子在不同生活情景下，体验情境式英语学习。故事应情境丰富、情节生动、充满趣味，简单但是有一定的深度，具有独特的育人价值，培养学生的文化意识和思维品质。低年级和中年级的学生，故事题材的选择偏重叙述类且和学生的日常生活紧密联系的内容，例如 *My Lucky Day* 和 *Something from Nothing*。

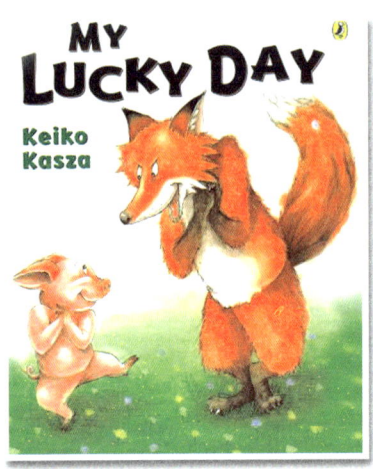

为高年级的学生选择故事时，注意题材类型的丰富性，既要选择一些 fiction 类型，也要选择一些 nonfiction 类型，体现学科融合，拓宽知识面。

（2）故事的情节。

学生心智发展是一个循序渐进的过程，因此，故事情节的选择也应由简单到复杂，符合不同年龄阶段学生的心理发展过程。对于低年级的故事教学，应选择情节相对简单、句式复现率高的故事。例如培生英语预备级里有很多故事都是同一句式反复出现，如 *My Cushion* 和 *At the Vet*。重复的句式便于孩子记忆，孩子不会感觉困难，能增加阅读兴趣、培养自信。

而对于中年级和高年级的故事教学，可选择情节起伏的故事，吸引学生的注意力，激发学生的阅读兴趣。如一些分级绘本中的较高级别文章。

My Cushion! My Cushion!
No, my cushion! No, my cushion!
No, my cushion! No, my cushion!
Oh no! My cushion!

My pet is a dog. My pet is a cat.
My pet is a rabbit. My pet is a rat.
My pet is a parrot. My pet is ... a spider!

（3）故事的篇幅。

故事的篇幅应长短适宜，与学生的年龄匹配，符合儿童对事物的理解能力和学习能力，生词量一般不宜超过10%。例如 The School Trip 对于四年级学生来说生词量过多，The Very Hungry Caterpillar 内容对于六年级学生来说过于简单幼稚。

此外，基于"以学生为主体"的教育理念，故事的选择可在一定程度上参考学生的意愿。一方面，教师可以通过问卷、调查、试读等方式了解学生的喜好，灵活选择故事。另一方面，学生可以根据年龄、性别、年级、阅读习惯、兴趣爱好、生活环境等选择适合自己的故事，实现自己的个性发展。

二、常用教学方法与活动

故事教学常用教学方法与活动主要有图片环游、拼图阅读、故事地图、阅读圈和持续默读等。

（一）图片环游

图片环游（Picture Tour）是师生共读故事、分享心得、合作探究故事意义的过程。教师引导学生观察封面、封底、扉页和文内图片，通过问题启发学生不断进行预测、推测和思考，在读中发现问题、分析问题、解决问题，同时分享生活经验。图片环游通常由以下几个步骤组成：热身导入、文本概念、图片环游、总结评价、默读与朗读、互动与分享。

1. 热身导入

通过游戏、歌曲歌谣、图片、视频等引入故事主题，激活学生已有知识经验，激发学生阅读兴趣。

案例一

活动名称：Listen and sing

活动意图：通过歌曲引入主题，激活学生已有的知识经验，激发阅读兴趣。

活动内容：教师播放歌曲"Let's go shopping"，学生第一遍听歌曲，第二遍唱歌曲，再说说歌曲中有哪些商店。

案例二

活动名称：Brain storming

活动意图：通过头脑风暴激活学生已有知识经验，锻炼学生观察能力和发散思维。

活动内容：猜猜故事里会有哪些动物。

2. 文本概念

引导学生关注封面、封底、扉页，了解标题、作者、插图作者等信息，培养学生的文本概念意识。

案例

活动名称：Look and say

活动意图：关注封面、扉页，了解标题、作者、插图作者等信息，培养文本概念意识。

活动内容：Show the cover page. Introduce the title, the writer and the illustrator.

师生展开对话如下：

T:　Who do you see on the cover page?

S1: I see a boy.

T:　He is David. What is David doing?

S1: He is tiptoeing on the books to reach for the fish tank. How dangerous!

T:　What's the title of the story?

Ss: No, David.

T:　Who wrote and drew the story?

S2: David Shannon.

T:　Look! This is David Shannon. He has written many books. Look! *David Goes to School, David Gets in Trouble.* You can read them if you like.

T:　Look at the end paper. Who is she?

S2: I think she is mom because she is angry. She said, "No, David."

T:　Maybe she is mom. Why is she so angry? Let's read the story together.

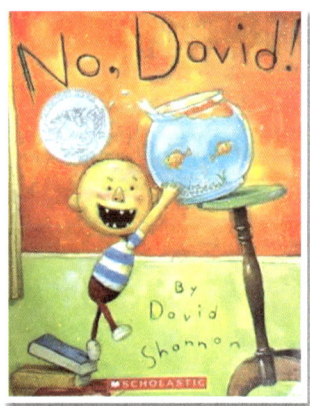

3. 图片环游

通过提出问题推动学生不断进行预测、推测和思考，梳理故事情节，理解人物情感，引领学生发现问题、分析问题、解决问题的同时分享生活经验。以故事教学 *Frogs in the Pool* 为例，在阅读故事的第一部分时教师采取图片环游的方式，在这一过程中教师不断提问引导学生阅读文本、寻求答案，在不断猜测和验证的过程中理解故事。针对每一幅图教师引导如下：

P2–P3: This is a family. This is dad. Dad asks, "Where are you going?" Mum answers, "I'm hot. I'm going for a swim." Where did you swim? Guess, where is mum going for a swim? Let's look at the next picture and check.

P4–P5: Mum went to the ... Yes, mum went to the pool. Can mum swim in the pool? Why or why not? No, because there are so many frogs. Mum shouted, "Frogs, frogs in the pool." Guess what would mum do? Let's look at the next picture.

P6–P7: Mum waved the towel and shouted, "Go away!" The frogs went ... Croak! Croak!

Croak!

P8−P9: Then mum put the frogs in a big net and said, "You are not swimming in my pool!" Will mum kill the frogs? No. Maybe mum will put the frog somewhere. Let's look at the next picture and check.

P10−P11: Mum went down the road. Is she tired? Finally she found a pool. She said, "Here's a pool. It is a pool for frogs." So she put the frogs into the pool. Are the frogs happy in the pool? Is mum happy, too?

4. 总结评价

教师引导学生总结故事、评论故事,可以评价人物、评论观点和做法,也可以谈论最喜欢的角色、最喜欢的故事情节等。注意问题的设计要有开放性,有利于发展学生的思维能力。

5. 默读与朗读

为了加深对文本的理解,对故事有完整的阅读体验,采用边听边读、独立默读、跟读、结伴朗读等多种形式默读、朗读故事。

6. 互动与分享

读完故事以后,学生可以结合自己的生活经验,交流自己的感受,表达自己的观点,提出自己的建议,续写故事结尾等。形式可以是写一写、演一演、唱一唱、做一做、画一画等。

(二)拼图阅读

拼图阅读(Jigsaw Reading)就是将拼图的理念运用到阅读中,把零散的阅读材料拼成完整的语篇。拼图阅读方式能激发阅读兴趣,提高合作能力、信息加工能力和逻辑思维能力。

以故事 The Hug 为例,在阅读故事的第二部分时教师不再进行图片环游,而是提出开放式的问题,引导学生思考、讨论、分享观点。Could Moosling give Pins a hug? What would Moosling do?学生在图片的帮助下,预测故事情节、推理故事的发展;接着呈现打乱顺序的图片,要求学生给图片合理排序。学生需要通过仔细观察图片、阅读文字、交流讨论来推理故事的情节发展,为图片排出合理的顺序。

以故事 *A House for Hedgehog* 为例，教师设置How，What等问题，引导学生预测后来小刺猬怎样了，接着呈现打乱顺序的句子，要求学生观察图片、阅读文字、合理排序。

Discuss and order
看图给句子排序。

What happened to Hedgehog?

( )So Hedgehog went back to his own house.

( )On the way, he slipped.

( )He got covered in leaves.

( )Hedgehog rolled and rolled.

再以故事 *The Very Hungry Caterpillar* 为例，学生阅读完故事前半部分后，猜测 What did the caterpillar eat?然后带着问题将打乱顺序的图片和文字合理排序。学生可以依据图片和文本中的日期、食物数量等线索完成排序。

one lollipop,one piece of cherry pie,one sausage,one cupcake,and one slice of watemelon.

On Saturday he ate through one piece of chocalate cake,one ice-cream cone,one pickle,one slice of Swiss cheese,one slice of salami,

That night he had a stomachache!

On Monday he ate through one apple,

But he was still hungry.

On Tuesday he ate through two pears,

But he was still hungry.

On Thursday he ate through **four** strawberries,
But he was still hungry.

On Friday he ate through **five** oranges,
But he was still hungry.

On Wednesday he ate through **three** plums,
But he was still hungry.

（三）故事地图

故事地图（Story Map）就是将阅读内容可视化、图形化、结构化，帮助学生梳理故事情节的发展脉络、理解故事价值意义。学生在教师的指导与帮助下，由文本主题出发，依据故事内容，梳理结构，完成图表、思维导图等。

以故事教学 *The Hug* 为例，在读后阶段教师呈现 Story Map，引导学生通过完成故事地图，梳理故事发生的地点、人物、事件、结果等要素，故事脉络清晰明朗。

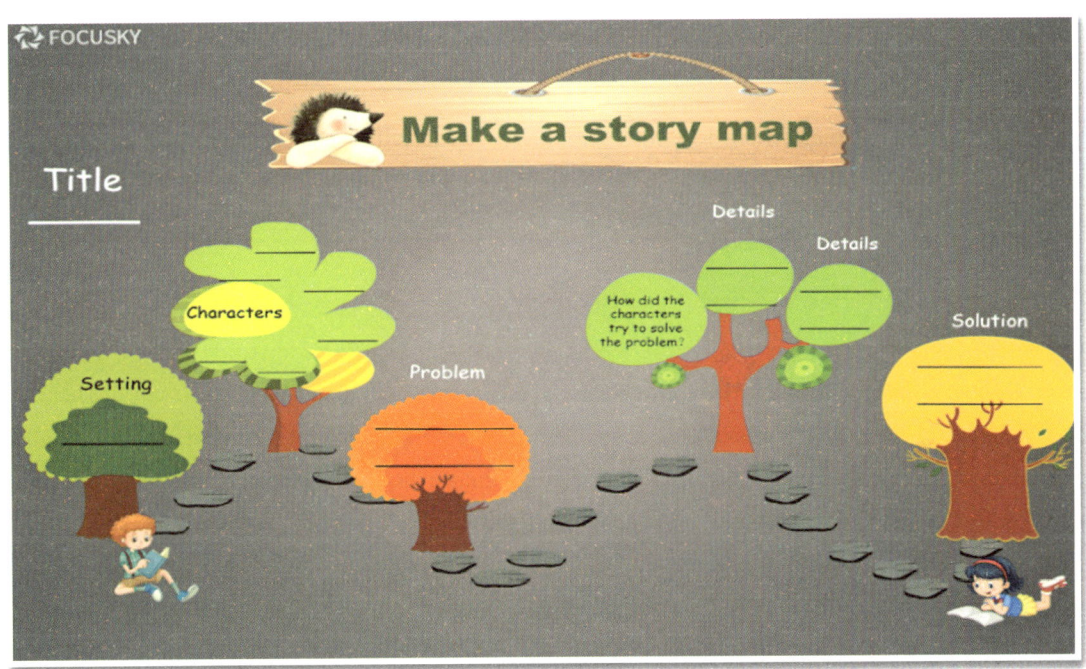

以故事教学 *Rapunzel* 为例,在读后阶段教师将阅读内容图表化,呈现如下表格,引导学生用所给单词和句子完成表格,明确故事名称、作者、人物、故事发生的地点、过程等,故事要素一目了然。

Fill in the blanks.用所给单词和句子完成表格

Name of the story（故事名）	Rapunzel
Author（作者）	Ellis.p （艾丽斯）
Characters（人物）	a girl a young man the girl's father
Settings（地点）	castle the girl's house
Process（过程）	1. The young man hears the princess.
	2. The young man climbs up.
	3. They climb down the rope.
	4. They get on the man's white horse.

（四）阅读圈

阅读圈(Reading Circles)是小组成员按照分工完成任务,开展合作阅读的一种活动。它能提高学生的阅读能力、思辨能力以及合作学习能力。

阅读圈活动一般分工为:组长负责针对故事提问,组织小组成员讨论并发表意见和见解;生活联系者负责将故事中的内容与自身生活相联系,发表感想和体验;总结者负责对故事作简短总结;文化联系者负责寻找和对比故事中出现的与中国文化的异同现象;单词解释者负责解释文中的新词,并将新词用于真实的句子中;名句发现者负责寻找和分享有意义的句子、段落或优美的语言。然后,组长组织组员进行组内交流和分享,汇报任务完成情况,阐述对阅读材料的理解。最后,小组自愿向全班进行展示。

（五）持续默读

持续默读(Sustained Silent Reading)指学生在一个时间段内不受其他事情干扰、独立自主的阅读,通常是10—15分钟,而且读后不需要接受测试或进行汇报等。持续默读能让学生在毫无压力的情况下接触阅读,逐渐养成良好的阅读习惯。

三、教学片段模拟训练

片段一

外研社多维英语第3级: Hide and Seek

图片环游:

Part 1: (P14−P15) Tiger was hurt. There were so many thorns in his head and legs.

Ss listen to the voice and guess. What's wrong with Tiger?

【设计意图】引导学生通过听音频,猜测故事结尾,设置悬念,激发学生阅读下去的兴趣。

Part 2: (P4−P11) Monkey looked for Tiger under the rock, under the log and in the leaves.

1. Ss read P4−P11 and find out. How many places did Monkey look for? Where are they?

2. Look and find P4–P5. Where was the tiger?

3. Read and find P6–P11. Where was the tiger?（完成表格）

4. Check the answers.

【设计意图】设置情境，引导学生有效地进行信息输出，培养学生对语言的实际运用能力。及时进行反馈和评价，激发学生阅读故事的欲望。

Part 3: (P14–P15) Monkey helped Tiger.

Ss read and understand. We should be kind and helpful when someone was hurt.

Don't do things rashly. We should be more careful.

【设计意图】情感升华，明确故事的核心价值，即乐于助人和谨慎做事的道理。

案例视频

（滕州市第二实验小学 孙　静）

片段二

外研社多维英语第3级: No Kings in the Kitchen

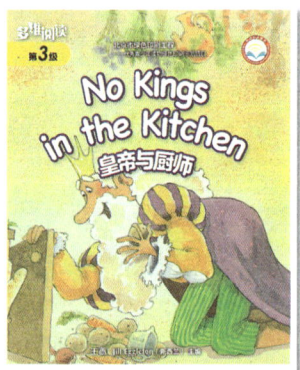

拼图阅读：

Part 3: (P11–P15) The kitchen is on fire. The cook puts the water on fire. The king is pushed away from the kitchen.

1. Let Ss work in groups (4 students in a group). Each group will be given 4 pages

(disordered) of the story. Ss read all the 4 pages within groups to understand the story and put them in order.

What happened next? What did the cook say? Did the cook say "Silly king" aloud? Why? What did the king say?

2. Choose one group to read the 4 pages in order in front of the class. Then choose some Ss to give the answer of their group.

3. Lead Ss know the end of the story. Is this story real?

【设计意图】通过拼图阅读的方式能够充分调动学生的参与度,在图片及文本的帮助下梳理故事情节,将文本合理排序,提升学生的分析判断与逻辑思维能力。小组合作、共同展示的形式能够帮助学习有困难的学生,使其基本掌握故事内容。小组讨论后,对单个同学的提问一定程度上也促进了个人自主能力的发展。

案例视频

（滕州市荆河街道中心小学
刘　帅）

四、范例导读

【教学内容】海尼曼分级阅读G2（Level E）The Hug
【设　计　者】滕州市木石镇峭村小学　刘华东

Little Pins wanted a hug.
"A hug will feel good,"
she said.
"Will you hug me, Mouse?"

"I want a hug," Pins said.
"Will you hug me, Hoot?"

"Come here, Pins," said Hoot.
"You can play my drum."

"That will make you happy,"
said Mouse.

"I wish I could get a hug!"
said Pins.
"Will you hug me, Skunk?"

"I can't!" said Skunk.
"Do you want to shake hands?"

Moosling went to Rabbit.
He got Rabbit to
take off his jacket.

"Moosling! Moosling!" Pins said.
"Will **you** give me a hug?"

11

13

Then Moosling gave little Pins
a big, big hug.

15

【案例说明】

本课为故事教学课,教学内容选自海尼曼分级阅读G2(Level E),这一系列旨在通过引人入胜的阅读内容激发学生的阅读兴趣,促使他们养成自主阅读的习惯,为以后展开深入系统的英语阅读奠定良好的基础。故事The Hug主要讲述了小豪猪Pins想要得到一个拥抱,但是朋友Mouse、Hoot、Skunk都怕Pins身上的刺儿扎伤自己,不敢给她拥抱。但是他们没有转身离开,而是想方设法逗Pins开心,跟她握手、让她打鼓玩。Pins并没轻言放弃,最终在Moosling的帮助下得到了拥抱。故事情节曲折生动,引发思考。故事语言结构重复,有利于学生熟悉并掌握目标语言,学会得体地向他人提出请求以及委婉地拒绝别人。通过阅读本故事可以提高学生的思维品质,培养独立思考、解决生活实际问题的能力;通过分析人物对话,评价人物行为,挖掘人物性格,学会得体的表达和交流,提高学生品格修养。

【教学流程】

Warm up and lead-in	Free talk Look and say
Presentation and practice	Part 1:(P2-P7) Feel the change of Pins' words she asked Part 2:(P8-P10) Observe the pictures and say/Think and evaluate the characters/Think and say Part 3:(P11-P16) Think, discuss and share/Do jigsaw reading in groups
Consolidation	(1) Enjoy the whole story (2) Discuss in groups and say/share (3) Make a story map in groups (4) Act the story
Homework	Read other stories in Moosling series

【教学设计】

（一）知识与技能目标

1. 学生能够在图片的帮助下读（听）懂故事，理清故事要素，如人物、背景、情节、问题、解决方法等。

2. 学生能够表演和创编故事。

3. 学生能够得体地提出请求以及委婉地拒绝别人，如：Will you ...? Yes, I will./I wish I could./I can't.

4. 学生能够基于故事展开合理的预测和推理，针对问题的解决展开发散思维。

（二）情感态度目标

1. 能够理解和体会Pins心怀梦想并且为实现梦想坚持不懈的精神。

2. 能够体会朋友们的善良体贴以及Moosling的热情、机智、乐于助人的优良品质。

（三）学习策略目标

1. 通过听故事、读故事、讲故事，理解故事，获取基本信息。

2. 通过评故事、演故事、编故事（适合学习程度较好的学生）进一步理解和体会故事。

【教学准备】

课件、绘本人物图片、词卡、两块黑板、绘本、Story map、Jigsaw Reading卡片

【教学过程】

Step 1　Before-reading

1. Greetings.

Do the chicken dance.

2. Look and say.

Say the animals they see quickly.

【设计意图】激活旧知，引出故事主要人物。

3. Cover page.

(1) Show the cover page.

Introduce the main characters and the title.

Ss read the title and say the main characters.

(2) Elicit Ss' prediction.

T: Where are they?/Who wanted a hug? Pins or Moosling?/Why do you think so?/Could Moosling give Pins a hug?/If Pins and Moosling hug together, what might be happening?

Ss predict the story according to their own background.

【设计意图】观察封面，从标题图片等处提取信息，了解故事人物以及故事发生的背景。使用"猜测和预测"策略，根据图片的提示预测故事情节，展开合理的想象，激发阅读兴趣。

Step 2　While-reading

Part 1: (P2–P7) Pins asks Mouse, Hoot, and Skunk for a hug.

1. Elicit Ss to listen and say.

T: What did Pins say?

Students listen to Page 2 and answer the questions.

【设计意图】通过听故事,初步感受主人公一开始的心情,为之后分析故事人物情感变化做铺垫。

2. Elicit Ss to read P3–P7 and find out the answers.

T: Who did Pins ask for a hug?/Did they give little Pins a hug? Why?/How did Pins ask her friends?

Students read and answer the questions.

【设计意图】通过分析人物对话,体会人物情感变化,挖掘人物性格。学生在阅读过程中使用归纳、比较等策略分析并体会人物情感。通过仿读,进一步体会和表达人物情感。

3. Check the answers.

T: When Pins asked Mouse, how did Pins feel?/Mouse and Hoot couldn't give Pins a hug, how did Pins feel?/Skunk couldn't give Pins a hug, how did Pins feel?

Students think and say.

Happy-sad-very sad (disappointed)

【设计意图】通过分析故事语言,体会故事人物的心理变化。

4. Elicit Ss to feel the change of Pins' words she asked.

Students practice with their partners with expression.

Will ...

I want ...Will you ...

I wish I could ...Will you ...

T: Did they want to give Little Pins a hug? How do you know?

【设计意图】通过两人模仿对话,进一步体会故事人物的心理变化。

Part 2: (P8–P10) Mouse, Hoot and Skunk want to help Pins be happy.

1. Observe the pictures and say.

T: What did Pins' friends do?

【设计意图】引导学生仔细观察图片信息。

2. Read P8–P9 and say.

T: What did they say?

3. Check the answers.

T: Why did they do these things?

4. Evaluate the characters.

T: What do you think of Pin's friends?

【设计意图】引导学生读故事,通过分析人物对话,评价人物行为,理解和体会朋友们的言行。评价人物性格,体会朋友们善良体贴、乐于助人的优良品质,培养学生的共情心。

5. Look and say.

T: After playing the drum, did Pins feel good? Why/Why not?

6. Think and say according to the story.

T: Have you ever been refused by others? How did you feel then? What happened?

【设计意图】引导学生运用元认知策略调动自身背景知识来理解故事。联系学生生活实际,引发思考。

Part 3: (P11–P16) Pins asks Moosling for a hug.

1. Listen and say.

T: What did Pins do next?/Could Moosling give Pins a hug?/What did he say?

2. Think, discuss and share.

T: What would Moosling do?

【设计意图】开放性问题能够培养学生的发散思维。在图片的帮助下预测故事情节,推理故事的发展。

3. Do the Jigsaw Reading in groups.

T: What did Moosling do?

Students in groups read the sentences and look at the pictures carefully, then order.

【设计意图】通过小组合作,仔细阅读文字、观察图片了解故事的结局。

4. Check the answers.

First ... Second ... Third ... At last ...

Think and say.

【设计意图】发挥学生多元智能优势,总结并概括故事片段。

Step 3　After-reading

1. Read the whole story silently.

2. Enjoy the whole story.

3. Discuss in groups and say/share.

T: Who is your favorite character? Why? (What can you learn from this story?)

【设计意图】通过评价故事人物,达成德育教学目标。

4. Make a story map.

Students in each group try to make a story map according to their understandings.

【设计意图】通过此活动引导学生梳理整个故事的脉络。

5. Act the story.

Students act the story with their understandings.

【设计意图】提升语言综合运用能力,体会故事中人物的感受,进一步理解故事所蕴含的意义。

Step 4　Homework

Read other stories in Moosling series.

【设计意图】推荐阅读书目,拓展阅读空间。

【板书设计】

【设计思路】

　　故事 The Hug 情节曲折生动,容易引发学生思考;故事语言结构重复,有利于学生熟悉并掌握目标语言并学会得体地向他人提出请求以及委婉地拒绝别人。故事内容符合学生的认知水平且生动、有趣,符合学生的兴趣特点。在引导学生获得知识的同时,教师还注重通过感知、联系自身生活实际等创设多样化的教学活动,引发学生思考,在师生真实交流中促进学生思维和表达能力的发展。在教学的不同阶段,教师采用不同的阅读方式、提出不同的问题与任务,引导学生主动、积极地思考。比如,教师让学生设身处地地思考主人公被拒绝后的心情、谈论自己被拒绝的经历等,不仅激发了学生的参与热情,还在潜移默化中培养了学生的同理心。在回顾总结阶段,教师通过引导学生完成故事地图的方式梳理了故事发生的地点、人物、事件、结果等,让学生对整个故事的发展脉络更加清晰明了。在板书方面,教师利用一块黑板呈现了故事情节发展的脉络图,另外一块白板呈现引导学生阅读文本的学习策略及问题,既有利于直观理解文本内容,又有助于学生学习策略的培养。

案例视频

(滕州市木石镇峭村小学
刘华东)

五、课后训练

根据外研社多维阅读第3级 Crazy Cat 写一份教学设计并试讲。

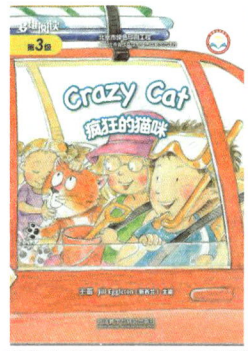

- 了解语法的功能
- 了解语法教学基本内容
- 理解语法教学的原则与策略
- 运用常用教学方法组织教学

一、语法教学概述

语法是系统地整合语言单位的有效工具,是语言能力的重要组成部分,是规范、准确和逻辑表达英语的基础。其实质是用形式化、程式化的手段来组织语义、语用信息。著名语言学家Wilkins(1983)曾指出,"对一种语言语法体系的习得依然是语言学习中的一个重要环节,语法是获得语言运用创造性的手段,缺乏语法知识会严重影响交际能力"。可见任何一种语言都有其特定的规则。学习英语如果不能了解它的内部规则,终究会影响学生准确地、成功地运用语言进行交流。

然而在日常小学英语语法教学活动中,教师对语法教学的认识存在很大的争议,在语法教学中出现了两种比较极端的做法。一种是过度重视语法,使得语法教学形式化、孤立化。教师在课上集中讲解,把相关语法点详细地讲给学生,然后学生大量操练。另一种是忽略语法,认为语法知识可有可无,采取"视而不见"的态度。很显然这两种做法都对小学英语语法教学的认识有失偏颇。语法教学是要将语法规则和语法意义教学结合起来。语法教学不能局限在对语法规则的讲授和操练上,不能只注重语法结构和形式,还要重视语法意义教学,否则即使学生掌握了语法规则也不能正确地使用。

小学阶段对于英语语法教学的基本要求有相关阐述。

级 别	内 容 要 求
一 级	1. 在语境中感知、体会常用简单句的表意功能 2. 在语境中理解一般现在时和现在进行时的形式、意义、用法 3. 围绕相关主题,在语境中运用所学语法知识描述人和物,进行简单交流

（续表）

级　别	内　容　要　求
二　级	1. 在语篇中理解常用简单句的基本结构和表意功能 2. 在语境中理解一般过去时和一般将来时的形式、意义、用法 3. 在语境中运用所学语法知识描述、比较人和物,描述具体事件的发生、发展和结局,描述时间、地点和方位等

基于《义务教育英语课程标准(2022年版)》的阐述可以得到以下几点启示:第一,语法教学应创设丰富的语境,在理解和表达活动中帮助学生习得语法知识。语言与学习者的真实生活密不可分,语言的发展是在自然真实的语境中通过与他人展开交流获得的,无法通过脱离语境机械重复的操练而获得。第二,在语言使用中,语法知识是"形式-意义-使用"的统一体。语法教学应遵循形式意义和使用统一的原则,让学生感知和体验形式与意义的联系,在语境中运用所学语法进行交流和表达。

整个小学阶段的语法教学都不是为培养学生掌握一系列复杂的语法术语、概念和用语法分析语言的能力的,而是从语用的角度去讲语法,围绕这一目的,教师不把语法教学作为主要教学内容,不去专门教语法,而是在大量生动、直观、有趣、富有交际性的语言活动中学习,做到小学语法教学的"淡化而不忽略,重视而不过分"。

二、教学原则与策略

无规矩不成方圆,小学英语语法教学也有其基本教学原则。小学英语语法教学要求教师采用适合儿童身心发展规律的教学方式,在遵循语法教学的基本原则的前提下,把语法教学分层次、分步骤地向前推进,让学生在语境中感知语法,在活动中学习语法,在训练中巩固语法,在运用中提升语法。小学英语语法教学需遵循以下原则。

1. 隐性原则

隐性的语法教学原则是指在教学中避免直接谈论所学的语法规则,它是相对于显性的语法教学原则而言的。隐性的语法教学是让学生尽量少直接接触抽象晦涩的语法术语,而通过创设教学情境用一定的语句、活动、直观教具等形式,让学生在观察、模仿、体会和运用中学习语法,从而从心理上学起语法更轻松、更自如。因此教师要创设一定的语言情境让学生体验语言,通过对语言的交际性运用归纳出语法规则。教师可以利用儿歌、故事、游戏等间接的方法来帮助学生学习语法。

比如PEP《英语(三年级起点)》三年级下册第五单元中出现的可数名词复数语法项目,教师可以采用Let's chant部分进行语法教学。歌谣节奏感强、朗朗上口,有利于激发学生的学习兴趣。学生在节奏鲜明、富于韵律感的歌曲童谣中学习语法,能起到事半功倍的效果。

这首歌谣叙述了小熊Zoom贪吃水果的故事,把歌词中出现的apples, grapes, bananas, oranges和pears复数形式形象地展现在学生面前。歌谣一共有六句话,第三句和第六句歌词

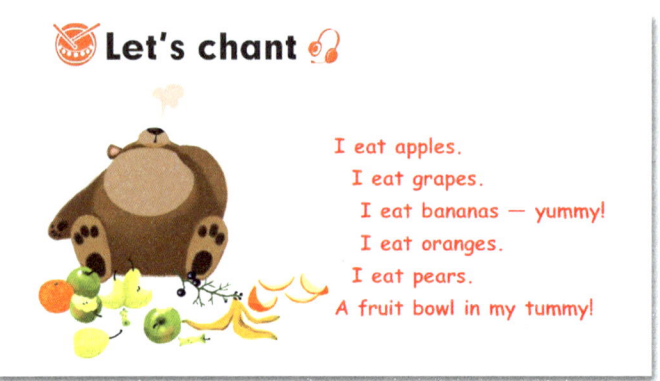

分别用yummy和tummy结尾,增加了歌谣的韵律感。通过学唱这首歌谣,既发展了学生的语言能力,也发展了学生利用歌谣进行语法理解记忆的能力。

2. 意义先行原则

意义先行原则是指先意义再形式。在小学英语语法教学中,不能让语法结构的学习先入为主,应该先让学生在一个有意义的情境中理解语法意义,然后给学生提供机会在真实的语境中运用语法知识进行交际活动,最后,教师把学生的注意力吸引到语法规则上来,完成由面到点的转化,从而进一步巩固所学知识,形成一个完整的知识网络。

心理学研究表明,如果学生所听到的和所看到的是在一定情境之中使用的语言,其基本句型结构通过反复使用,反复操练,他们就会达到不假思索地脱口而出的程度。因为真实、恰当的教学情境能够帮助学生更好地理解语法意义,教师在语法教学中要利用图片、动画、实物、简笔画、肢体语言等直观教具或手段把抽象的语法知识生动地呈现在学生面前。教师要带领学生将语法结构放在具体情境中操练,才会让语法教学更有意义、更直观、更有趣生动,才不会让学生感到枯燥乏味。以PEP《英语(三年级起点)》五年级上册Uint 5 There is a big bed中的Let's talk教学片段为例。

T: Look at the picture. Whose room is it?

[设计意图] 引导学生观察图片，让学生在一个有意义的情境中理解语法意义。

Ss: This is Zhang Peng's bedroom.

T: How do you know that?

S1: A photo.

T: You are right. There is a photo of Zhang Peng. I like his room. It's nice. What is in the room?

[设计意图] 让学生通过教师的语言初步感知 There be 语法项目的用法和语言意义。

S2: A bed.

T: Yes. There is a bed. Look at the picture again. There is a ...

S3: There is bike.

T: Yes! There is a bike. There is a bike. Come on, children. There is a ...

[设计意图] 学生刚一开始不会使用 There be 来表达自己的想法，只能说出一个单词，或者在表达的时候会出现这样那样的语法错误。教师没有直接纠正，而是耐心示范，不断重复，把自己的语言变成学生学习语法的资源，适时引导、鼓励学生大胆表达。

S4: There is a clock.

T: Wonderful! There is a clock.

S5: There is a computer.

T: Perfect! What is in our classroom?

[设计意图] 教师用教室里的真实情境作为语境，进一步强化和构建这个时态的用法和语言意义的联系。经过反复的练习和实践，学生已经能够用 There be 句型熟练地表达自己的想法了。

S6: There is a blackboard.

S6: There is a TV.

　　通过以上教学片段不难看出，教师在教学 There be 语法项目的过程中，没有直接讲解该语法项目的结构与形式，而是先让学生通过仔细观察图片参观张鹏的卧室，在有意义的情境中体会 There be 的语法意义，感知 There be 句型的语义及语用功能。接下来将教学情境植入学生的班级，让学生在真实的语境中运用 There be，完成了由虚拟情境到真实情境的过渡。教师将陌生的 There be 句型放到学生所熟知的 classroom 中学习，既增强了学习的趣味性，又降低了语法学习的难度。

3. 适时适量原则

适时适量原则就是指教师在语法项目的教学过程中要注意在什么时间讲、讲到什么程度，即选择合适的时机和学生进行交流分享。有些老师在教学过程中一遇到语法项目就开始滔滔不绝地解释，不放过任何一个语法点，唯恐语法项目影响了学生的理解能力；还有的老师错误地认为只有把语法项目解释透彻了，才能保证学生在英语学习的过程中不出错。教师在讲解语法项目时只要做到在最适宜的时候适当引导、在最关键的地方适当点拨即可，否则便会矫枉过正、弄巧成拙。

4. 循序渐进原则

任何一个语法项目都不是一次可以学会的，这就要求语法教学要渐进地、持续性地进行。循序渐进教学原则，是指教师按照科学知识内在的逻辑顺序和学生认知发展的顺序进行教学，使学生逐步地、系统地掌握基础知识和基本技能，并在此基础上促进发展。教师可以利用简笔画、图片等形式，根据学生的已有知识经验，选择一个适合的语篇或者借助相同的句式创编一个有趣的语篇，让学生通过模仿、体会和诵读，逐步理解语篇大意，循序渐进地知晓语法规则。

例如在学习 see 后面接动词的 ing 形式这一语法时，就可以借助绘本 *Brown bear, brown bear, what do you see?* 中的内容展开教学。绘本中的语言是这样的：Brown bear, brown bear, what do you see? I see a red bird looking at me. Red bird, red bird, what do you see? I see a yellow duck looking at me. Yellow duck, yellow duck, what do you see? ... 整个绘本语言的特点是结构简明，语句重复，框架清晰，有规律可循。绘本围绕学生身边所熟悉的人和物进行编写，涉及动物、颜色、老师和同学，故事情节虽然简单，但是每一个片段都与下一个片段紧密相连，一步一步地往前推进，给人的感觉是道路越走越宽阔，无穷无尽。故事从 brown bear 开始，一直围绕着动物和颜色往前推进，但是到了最后故事给人一种意想不到的收尾：Teacher, teacher, what do you see? I see children looking at me. Children, children, what do you see? We see a brown bear, a red bird, a yellow duck ... and a teacher looking at us. That's what we see. 教师引导学生模仿、跟读，几遍下来之后，学生渐渐地就能在图片的帮助下说出句子 I see a ... looking at me，在不知不觉中就学会了 see 后面接动词的 ing 形式这一语法项目。

5. 实践性原则

任何语言的学习都不能脱离实践和反复练习。同理，小学英语语法教学离不开真实的教学活动，否则就成了"无源之水，无本之木"。只有把语法知识运用到现实的语言交际中才能彰显其价值和意义。教师要引导学生通过反复不断的训练和实践，在具体的教学活动中感知、体会和运用语法知识。

以 PEP《英语（三年级起点）》六年级下册 Uint 4 Then and now 中的 Let's wrap it up 板块为例。Let's wrap it up 是一个教学活动，该活动要求学生通过观察组图的变化，根据图片的情境和语义说出恰当的语言形式。这些图片都是发生在学生身边的，是学生生活经验的一部分，学生能够对比出每组图片的变化，选择合适的时态来表达自己的想法。

6. 交际性原则

语言是自然发展的人类活动，是为了交际目的而存在的一种社会现象。语言不用来交际就失去了自身的意义。活学活用是语法学习的终极目的。语言学习的重点是真实话语或阅读文本的意义，而非语言本身。这就意味着把语言肢解为语音、词汇、语法等，然后孤立地进行单项训练是没有意义的。另外语言学习必须是以学习者为中心，学习的目的是体验完整使用的语言，来表达自己的思想，而不是鹦鹉学舌简单模仿。如果教师只注重传授单词、短语、句子的意思就容易"见木不见林"，保证不了学生对文本意义的整体把握。因此在语法教学活动中，教师要鼓励学生大胆尝试运用语法实现自己的交际目的，循序渐进、由简到难。教师对学生在尝试交流中出现的错误要给予宽容的态度，保护学生英语学习的自信心。

以 PEP《英语（三年级起点）》六年级上册 Unit 6 How do you feel? 中的 Let's learn 为例，本课的语法知识是使用句型 "What should I do? You should ..." 给他人提出适当的建议。在学生感知、体验、理解语法知识后，教师设计一份调查表，让学生在真实的情境中互相交流，并鼓励学生创编成对话，由句到篇，由听说到练习，层层递进，通过这种拓展性的练习强化学生的语法知识。

Name: _____	Age: ____
feelings	worried/happy/angry/sad
Advice	You should _____.

三、教学片段模拟训练

案 例

PEP《英语（三年级起点）》六年级下册 Unit 2 Last weekend 中的 Let's learn

【案例说明】

本单元的话题是"last weekend"，与学生的日常生活紧密联系，符合学生的生活实际。主要语言功能是能够在一定的情境和语境中询问他人上周末发生的事情以及对他人的询问做出回答。学生通过学习本单元，学会与他人分享上周末的经历，养成合理安排周末生活的好习惯。

本课时是第四课时，学生对于动词过去式的学习已经有了一定的基础。本部分教学通过 Amy 和 John 两人的对话展开，学习了表示过去时间的单词及短语，并在图片的帮助下学会用一般疑问句询问他人过去的行为并作出相应的回答。

【教学片段设计】

（一）教学目标

1. 学生能在 last weekend 语境中听、说、读、写词组 had a cold, slept, read a book, saw a film, last weekend/night/Monday, yesterday, the day before yesterday，进一步了解动词过去式的变化规则。

2. 学生能在 last weekend 语境中运用—Did you like it? —Yes, I did. 核心句型与他人展开交流。

3. 学生能进一步理解一般过去时的形式、意义和用法，并在真实的语境中正确运用该语法项目。

4. 以 John 和 Amy 两人关于周末活动的谈话为背景，通过描述和讨论，学生学会合理安排周末。

（二）教学重难点

动词过去式的变化，以及在特定语境下用一般过去时与他人交流。

（三）教具

图片、视频、多媒体课件

（四）教学过程

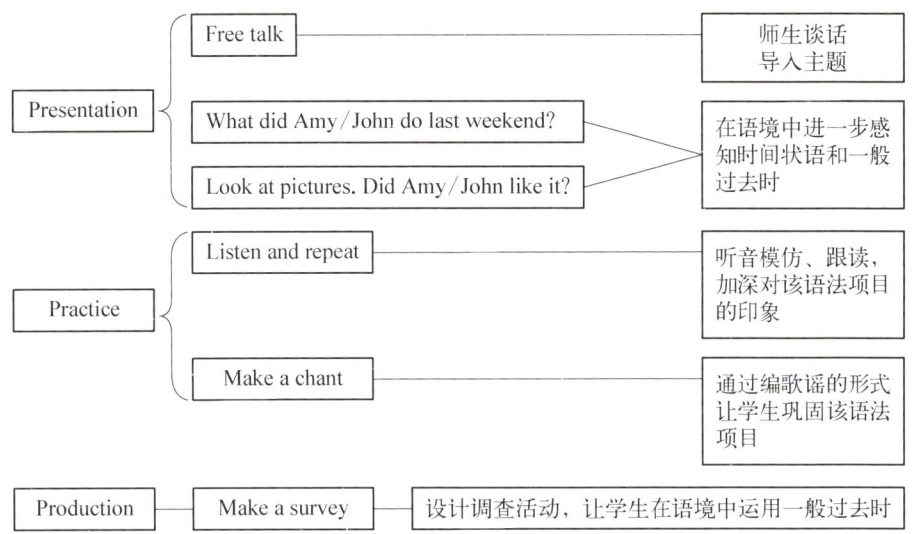

【设计思路】

本节课以 Amy 和 John 上周末的生活展开教学。教师能够整体把握教材，根据学生的实际情况，创设情境展开语法教学。在教学过程中教师没有给学生强调生僻的语法术语，如动词的过去式、规则变化和不规则变化等，而是通过 last weekend/night/Monday, yesterday, the day before yesterday 这些时间状语整体教授这一语法项目，让学生在 last weekend 语境中运用—Did you like it? —Yes, I did. 核心句型与他人展开交流。

在热身环节，通过复习建立新旧知识之间的联系。在呈现环节，通过 John 和 Amy 的对话，让学生在情境中感知表示过去的时间状语和一般过去时。练习环节，教师设计多种练习方式，如自己读、同伴读、小组读等把课堂还给学生，让学生训练语法、巩固语法。最后教师再创情境，让学生在一个全新的语言环境中正确运用所学的语法知识完成教学活动。这样的语法教学设计可以减少学生学习语法时的畏惧心理，降低语法学习的难度，帮助学生在一定的语境中学习语法、运用语法。

案例视频

（枣庄市峄城区匡衡小学
孟祥云）

四、范例导读

课文来源

PEP《英语（三年级起点）》五年级下册 Unit 5 Whose dog is it?

<h2>单元整体设计</h2>

（一）教材内容

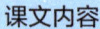

课文内容

（二）单元教学内容与要求

主题模块	学习内容		学习水平	学习与评价要求
1 语音	1.1 读音规则	1.1.1 字母组合ng和nk的发音规则	A	能够了解字母组合ng/nk的发音规则；能够读出符合ng/nk发音规则的单词，并能够根据发音拼写出符合ng/nk发音规则的单词
2 词汇	2.1 核心词汇：mine，yours，his，hers，theirs，ours，climbing，eating，playing，jumping，drinking，sleeping		C	能够听、说、读、写并在语境中正确使用mine，yours，his，hers，theirs，ours，climbing，eating，playing，jumping，drinking，sleeping
3 词法	3.1 代词	3.1.1 名词性物主代词	C	理解并运用名词性物主代词描述物品所属
	3.2 动词	3.2.1 动词现在分词	C	理解并运用动词的现在分词形式描述正在进行的动作
4 句法	4.1 句子时态	4.1.1 现在进行时	C	理解并运用现在进行时描述正在进行的动作
	4.2 句子种类	4.2.1 陈述句	C	用陈述句The yellow picture is mine.等句型描述物品的所属
		4.2.2 疑问句 — 4.2.2.1 特殊疑问句	C	用特殊疑问句Whose is it?进行提问，并回答It's ...'s.询问和回答某物属于某人
		4.2.2.2 一般疑问句	C	用一般疑问句Is he drinking water?进行提问，并回答Yes, he is./No, he isn't.用一般疑问句Are these all ours?进行提问，并用Yes, they are./No, they aren't.进行回答

（续表）

主题模块	学习内容			学习水平	学习与评价要求
4 句法	4.2　句子种类	4.2.2　疑问句	4.2.2.2　一般疑问句	C	用一般疑问句Can I play with him now? Can you take him to the park?进行提问,用以提出建议和征求许可
5 语篇	5.1　记叙文	5.1.1　基本信息	Read and write	B	故事基本信息的获得和描述
			Story time	A	简单讲述对话中的人物、地点、事件等基本信息

备注：A 知晓　B 理解　C 运用

（三）单元教学与评价目标

知识目标：

1. 能听、说、读、写mine, yours, his, hers, theirs, ours六个名词性物主代词,能够听、说、读、写climbing, eating, playing, jumping, drinking, sleeping六个动词现在分词。

2. 能在语境中听、说、读、写核心句型The yellow picture is mine. Whose is it? Are these all ours? Is he drinking water? No, he isn't. He's eating.

3. 能够了解字母组合ng/nk的发音规则,能够读出符合ng/nk发音规则的单词,并能够根据发音拼写出符合ng/nk发音规则的单词。

技能目标：

1. 能在情景中运用句型The yellow picture is mine. Are these all ours? Whose is it? It's Zhang Peng's. 询问和回答某物属于某人。用Is he drinking water? No, he isn't. 询问并回答某人正在做某事。

2. 能在语境中理解现在进行时的意义,正确运用现在进行时。

3. 能在语境中听懂、读懂语篇并提取相关信息,能够按照正确的意群及语音、语调朗读故事,并运用本单元所学核心句型复述故事,同时能够根据阅读所获信息写出故事梗概。

情感目标：

能够了解西方国家的宠物文化,感受中西方文化的异同。

（四）分课时教学与评价目标

课时与板块	知识与技能	语用与情感	评价活动
第一课时 Let's try Let's talk	1. 能完成听录音选择图片的活动,在图片和教师的帮助下理解对话大意 2. 能按照正确的语音、语调及意群朗读对话,并能进行角色表演	1. 能在语境中借助图文模仿演演对话,做到语言基本正确,表达比较流利	1. 根据图片提示预测听力内容,并选出正确答案

（续表）

课时与板块	知识与技能	语用与情感	评价活动
第一课时 Let's try Let's talk	3. 能在情景中运用句型：The ... is mine. Are these all ours? Whose is this? It's ...询问并回答某物属于某人	2. 能运用核心句型对物品的所属进行介绍	2. 流利朗读文本、正确运用核心句型展开交流
第二课时 Let's learn Look, say and complete	1. 能在一定的情境中听、说、读、写六个名词性物主代词：mine, yours, his, hers, theirs, ours 2. 能在语境中正确运用这六个单词及核心句型	能在语境中运用核心词汇与句型描述物品的所属	根据图片提示的意思，准确对应名词性物主代词和形容词性物主代词+名词
第三课时 Let's spell	能通过听例词发音，学习 ng 与 nk 在单词中的发音规则；能在录音的帮助下，强化记忆 ng 与 nk 的发音规则	1. 了解 ng 与 nk 在单词中的发音规则 2. 根据规则读出新单词、听录音圈单词、拼写单词	根据 ng 与 nk 的发音规则读出、拼出新单词
第四课时 Let's try Let's talk	1. 能在图片和教师的帮助下理解对话大意、朗读对话、表演对话 2. 能够在情景中运用句型 Is he ...? No, he isn't. He's ...询问并回答某人正在做某事 3. 能在语境中理解现在进行时的意义，正确运用现在进行时	1. 能在语境中借助图文模仿读演对话，做到语言基本正确，表达比较流利并且有一定情感 2. 能关心爱护动物	1. 能理解对话、操练对话、表演对话 2. 能在语境中运用核心句型与词汇进行交流
第五课时 Let's learn Let's play	1. 能在语境中听、说、读、写、运用六个动词的 -ing 形式 2. 能够掌握动词现在分词的变化规律 3. 能够运用核心句型完成组句游戏	1. 能正确使用六个动词的 -ing 形式描述正在进行的动作 2. 能根据图片预测听力内容	1. 根据图片提示描述正在进行的动作 2. 写出符合规律的动词的现在分词形式
第六课时 Read and write Let's check Let's wrap it up	1. 能够在图片的帮助下读懂短文，提取关键信息，提升阅读能力 2. 能够根据本节课所学，完成 Let's wrap it up 句子，并理解对话内容	了解机器人的功能	1. 读懂故事、表演故事、复述故事 2. 完成相关习题

课时教学设计

PEP《英语（三年级起点）》五年级下册 Unit 5 Whose dog is it? 中的 Let's talk

【设 计 者】枣庄市峄城区翰林小学　程宇

【教学流程】

Warm up
· Sing a song
· Free talk
· Listen and tick

Presenta-tion	·Look and answer. Watch and answer. Underline the key sentences. Read and answer. Listen and repeat.

practice	·Practice in pairs ·Read and complete ·Role play ·Summarize

Production	·Make a dialogue

【教学设计】

（一）教学目标

1. 能在听前预测听力重点，能运用听力技巧完成听力任务。

2. 能在语境中感知、理解对话内容并能借助图文模仿读演对话。

3. 能理解现在进行时的意义，运用核心句型 Is he doing ...? No, he isn't. He's doing ... 表达疑问，并做出相关回答。

4. 能够了解西方国家的宠物文化，感受中西方文化的异同。

（二）教学重难点

在语境中理解现在进行时这一语法项目的意义并在实际运用中体会其表意功能。

（三）教具准备

PPT、视频、图卡

（四）教学过程

Teaching steps	Teachers' activities	Purpose
I. Warm-up	1. Sing a song: 　*Animals, animals are everywhere.* 2. Free talk. 3. Listen and tick: where is the dog?	歌曲活跃气氛，师生谈话导入主题
II. Presentation	1. Look and answer. 　Who are they? Where are they? 2. Watch and answer. 　Where is Fido? 3. Underline the key sentences. 4. Read and answer. 　Sam will take him to the _____. 5. Listen and repeat.	引导学生通过观察图片、观看视频，在具体的语境中理解现在进行时的意义和用法

（续表）

Teaching steps	Teachers' activities	Purpose
III. Practice	1. Practice in pairs. 2. Read and complete. 3. Role play. 4. Summarize.	设计指向运用的活动，在实际运用中体会语法知识
IV. Production	Make a new dialogue. Mike: Come and look at my photo. We are in the nature park. Zhang Peng: Wow. There is a little dog. Mike: Yes, he is _____. Zhang Peng: Look at the cute rabbit. _____ _____ eating? Mike: No, she _____. She _____ playing with her friends. Zhang Peng: So lovely. I like the rabbit.	在情境中练习、巩固、运用语法项目的表意功能
V. Homework	Read the talk and try to recite.	
Blackboard Design		

【设计思路】

本课主要通过Sam到Chen Jie家做客时的问答来引导学生询问和回答某人或某物正在进行的动作，文本形式为对话，在对话的语言中涉及一般现在时的特殊疑问句。整个教学过程以隐性教学原则为主，引导学生在真实的语境中对现在进行时及其一般疑问句这一语法项目进行感悟、理解和初步运用，能够很好地实现"帮助学生知道常用的语法规则"这一目标。第一步，导

案例视频

（枣庄市峄城区翰林小学 程 宇）

入话题,感知对话文本,体会一般现在时的一般疑问句及其否定回答;第二步,分步突破,解读对话文本,理解一般现在时及其一般疑问句的意义;第三步,实际运用,提升对话文本,并在实际语境中尝试运用语法。

五、课后训练

根据PEP《英语(三年级起点)》五年级上册Unit 6 In a nature park中的Let's talk部分,撰写一份教学设计并试讲。

专题三

基本技能训练

模块一 英语书写

学习目标

- 能正确书写和使用大小写字母
- 能正确书写和使用常用标点符号
- 训练重点：
  英语字母书写笔顺和格位
  常用标点符号的使用
- 训练难点：
  书写倾斜度和间距
  书写速度

一、英语书写技能概述

随着多媒体在课堂上的广泛应用，英语教师在黑板上的板书越来越少，然而优美的线条滑过黑板的动态感和粉笔触及板面的特有声音是静止的屏幕文字无法替代的。书写不仅能够让我们体会到语言的美感与灵动，而且能够促进语言学习。英语书写训练分为钢笔字训练和粉笔字训练两类。钢笔字主要用在指导学生书写和批改作业时，粉笔字主要用在课堂教学中。教师的书写水平不仅影响着教学效果，而且无形中影响着学生的书写水平，甚至是书写态度、风格、习惯等。因此英语教师的书写训练是非常必要的。

英语书写练习字体的选择没有硬性要求，只要是自己想练、喜欢的字体都可以选择。英语书写常见练习字体有：手写印刷体、意大利体和圆体。手写印刷体是一种在外观上与印刷体十分相似的书写字体，也被称为英语的楷书字体。它的小写书写与汉语拼音在写法和外观上几乎完全相同，所以书写练习难度较低。意大利体也被称为英语的行书字体，是介于手写印刷体和圆体之间的一种字体。它兼具手写印刷体规矩、易于识别的特点和圆体流畅、迅速的优势，因此在书写实践中被广泛使用。我国小学英语课本上的书写体与意大利体非常接近，仅在细微处有些许差异。英语书写练习常见字体还有圆体，也称草体或花体。其特点是圆润、流畅，给人以飘逸柔美的感觉，令人赏心悦目。考虑到书写练习的渐进性，我们一般推荐先从临摹小学英语课本的字母开始练起，或者从手写印刷体或者意大利体练起。这三种书写体的共同特点是笔画结构简单,易识别,好上手,适合初学者练习。

英语字母(letters)不同于汉语的方块字(characters),两者书写练习用纸也有所差异。汉语信笺的设计是直线格或稿纸形式的方格纸,便于书写。而由英语字母构成的单词虽然呈横条形状,但具有上下延伸的特点。为了更好地掌握字母的延伸度,英语书写就采用了"四线三格纸"。所谓的"四线三格"就是四条横线构成的三道格。人们主要在第二道格里书写,也就是在第三条线上书写。

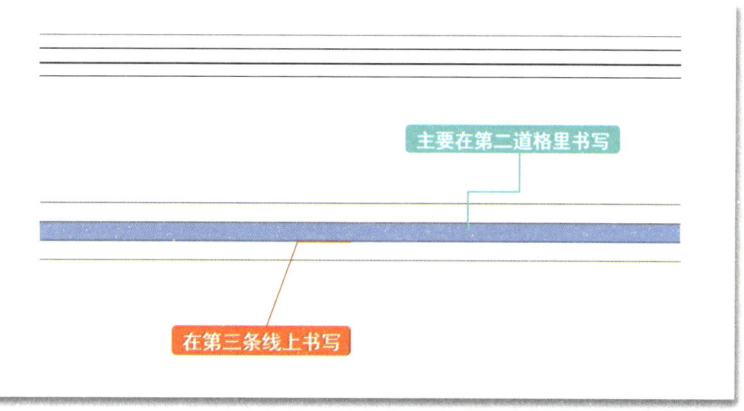

英语书写练习之初,我们可以借助四线三格辅助练习。参照课本的书写规范,勤加练习,久而久之,即使脱离了四线三格,也能写出格式规范的英语字母。

（一）字母笔顺和格位

英语字母是英语书写的基本单位。如同中国人在书写汉字时,要讲究书写规范,大小匀称、排列整齐。英语字母书写练习时,首先要确保字母笔顺和所占格位正确。比起复杂的汉字结构,英语的26个字母的笔顺较为简单,最多不会超过3笔,以横、竖和弯为主。

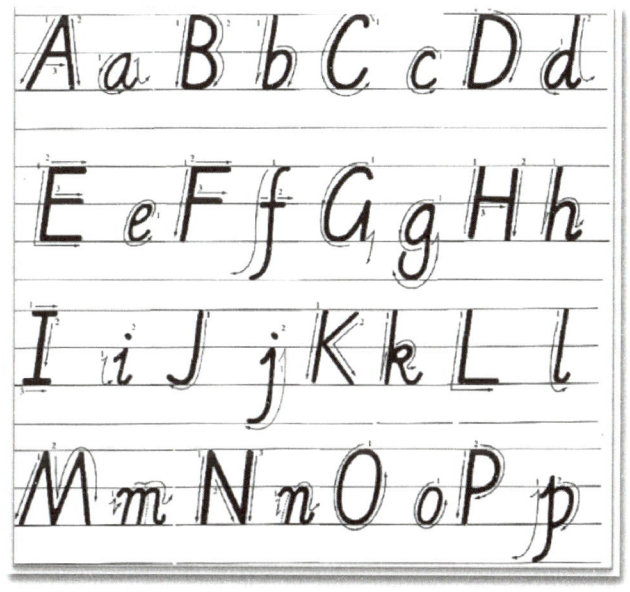

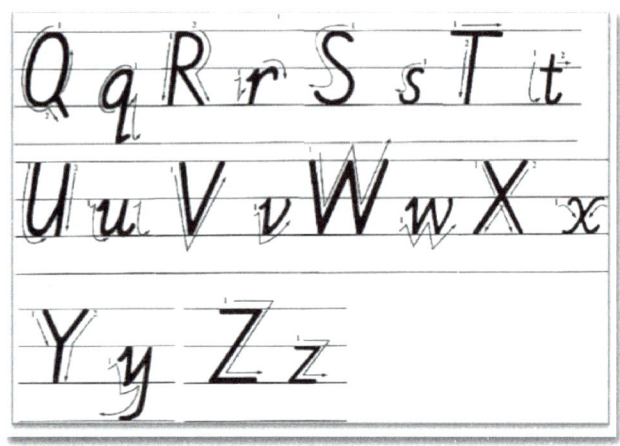

在书写的过程中注意大小写之分和所占格位。

1. 大写字母所占格位

所有的大写英语字母均占四线三格的上面两个格,即在第三道线上书写,要显得饱满。

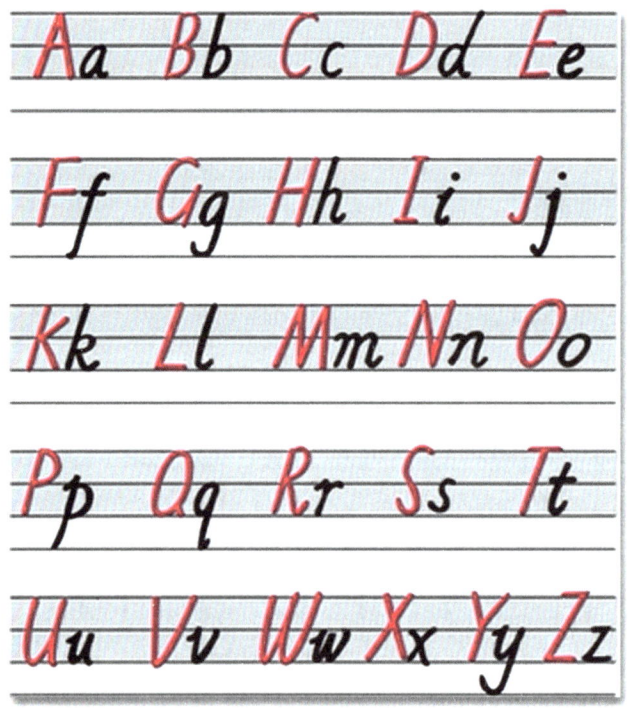

2. 小写字母所占格位

英语小写字母的书写就比较复杂了。根据书写特点,小写字母的书写可以分为四种情况:占一个格位;占上两个格位;占下两个格位;占满三个格位。

占一个格位,主要指在第三道线上书写,字母占满第二个格。包含的字母有:a,c,e,m,n,o,r,s,u,v,w,x,z 13个字母。

占上两个格位的字母有：b,d,h,i,k,l,t 7个字母。

占下两个格位的字母有：g,p,q,y 4个字母。

占满三个格位的字母有：f,j 2个字母。

（二）标点符号书写

标点符号是书面语言的有机组成部分。在英语学习中常用的标点符号是：句点、逗号、分号、冒号、问号、感叹号、连字符、撇号、省略号和双引号。

技能训练方法视频

（讲解人：李晓菲）

1. 句点

写法：写在句末单词的右下角。英语句号是小圆点，汉语句号是圆圈。

用法：

（1）用在一句话结束后的句末，表示一个句子的结束。

例如：There were many people there.

（2）用在某些缩略词之后，如：etc.

2. 逗号

写法：英语逗号的写法和汉语逗号相同。在四线三格第三线上写圆点，不要断笔。沿着圆点外圈的右侧向左出峰，注意横跨、近似平分第三线。

用法：

（1）用在并列连词（but、for、yet）前，用来连接句中的各分句。

例如：I'm sorry, but we didn't enjoy our stay very much.

（2）用来分割一系列单词、词组和从句。

例如：Head and shoulders, knees and toes, knees and toes.

（3）用来分割与句子其他部分密切相连的简短插入语或旁白。

例如：It's on the second floor. This way, please.

（4）用在修饰名词的多个形容词之间,或用在作表语的多个形容词之间。

例如：He's a tall, thin boy.

（5）用在写信中的称呼后。

例如：Dear Sir,

3. 分号

写法：分号是由一个实心点和一个逗号组成的。在四线三格中,首先顶着第二线下面写一个实心的圆点,再沿第三线上写一个逗号,出第三格。注意两者之间在第二格中是有空隙的。

用法：英汉分号写法相同,用法也一样。用于分割地位平等的独立子句,用在复合句内并列的分句之间。

例如：For the hard-working, a week has seven days; for the lazy, seven tomorrows.

4. 冒号

写法：首先是由两个实心的圆点组成,第一个顶在第二线下面,第二个写在离第三线稍微向上的位置,注意两点之间是有间隔的。

用法：

（1）用在被说明的词语之后。

例如：When: April 12th, 7 p.m.

（2）用在小时和分钟表达的数字中,把小时和分钟隔开。

例如：7：00 p.m.,6：00 a.m.

5. 问号

写法：问号写法与汉语问号相同,写在上两格。在第一格的二分之一处起笔,写一个向上走趋势的圆弧,然后再向向右下,经过第二线与起笔的点竖直,在第二格的三分之一位置收笔,沿着收笔竖直位置写一个实心的圆点,注意间隔。

用法：问号用法与汉语问号相同,用在疑问句句末。

例如：What would you like? Knife or fork?

6. 感叹号

写法：在第一格的三分之一处起笔,写一个斜竖,注意斜竖要拉直,在第二格离第三线的三分之一处收笔,然后在第三线上写一个实心圆点。注意斜竖和圆点的距离。

用法：

（1）用于加强命令语气或引起注意。

例如：Look! Mum, I'm hungry.

（2）表示感叹、赞美、嘲讽或开玩笑。

例如：What a great story!

7. 连字符

写法：在四线三格中第二个格中间位置,写一个短横。

用法：

（1）用于复合词。

例如：hard-working

（2）用于避免单词在语义或语音上发生混淆。

例如：ping-pong

（3）用于两个地名、两个数字或两个时间之间。

例如：It's eighty-five *yuan*.

8. 撇号

写法：在四线三格中，上顶第一线，不要断笔。沿着圆点外圈的右侧向左出峰。

用法：

（1）用于表示所有关系。

例如：the teacher's desk

（2）两个或多个单词缩写为一个词时，表示省略。

例如：didn't, don't

9. 省略号

写法：写在句末单词的右下角，下端紧靠第三线。英语的省略号是三个圆点。注意与汉语的省略号六个圆点的区分。

用法：

（1）表示省略。

例如：An English book, a math book, three storybooks and ...

（2）表示迟疑或犹豫。

例如：Shhhh ... Be quiet!

10. 双引号

写法：上顶第一线，不要断笔，沿着圆点外圈的左侧向右出峰。上顶第一线，不要断笔，沿着圆点外圈的右侧向左出峰。

用法：

（1）用于直接引语。

例如："Why is duck?" Little Duck asks.

（2）用于表示引起读者注意的词语。

例如：What's your name? How about "Max"?

二、技能训练方法

（一）基本笔画练习

英语字母书写练习前，先练习一些基本笔画，有利于尽快掌握英语书法的书写技能。笔画练习主要有四种：横的练习、斜线的练习、画圈的练习和弯钩的练习。

（1）横的练习。无论大写字母中的长横还是小写字母中的短横，都要写得水平。

（2）斜线的练习。英语书写具有一定斜度。书写时保持字母的斜度和间距一致，能达

到匀称美观的效果。

（3）画圈的练习。英语字母的形体圆润流畅，其书写与画圈有一定的相通之处。通过画圈练习学会控制手中的笔。当画圈的笔画运用游刃有余时，可以有意识地练习画半圆和椭圆，以便能直接运用于字母的书写。

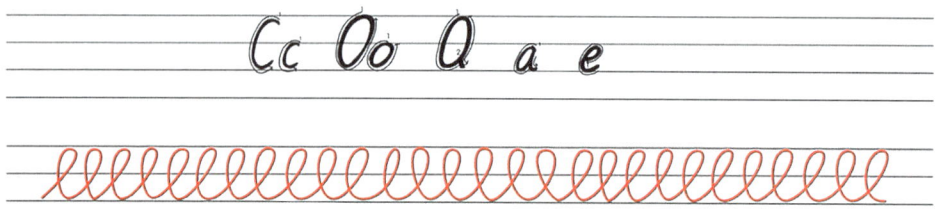

（4）弯钩的练习。弯钩是英语字母字形不可缺少的一部分，大多出现在字母起笔和收笔的位置。受汉语书写习惯的影响，弯钩笔画通常会误写成竖提，需要引起关注。

（二）分步练习操作

字母字形 ⇨ 字母笔顺 ⇨ 字母格位 ⇨ 字母高度 ⇨ 字母斜度 ⇨ 字母连写 ⇨ 字母间距
单词间距 ⇨ 句子行距 ⇨ 行间距

（三）保持横行平直的方法

1. 参照白纸或者黑板上边沿，尽可能保持相同距离，使第一行保持平直。

2. 参照白纸或者黑板左边沿，使横行与其保持垂直。

3. 板书时，将黑板分为2—3个部分，缩短黑板的左右距离，这样更容易把握每行字的平整。

三、书写方法与示例

1. 钢笔书写

2. 粉笔书写

技能训练方法视频

（讲解人：付玉伟）

技能训练方法视频

（讲解人：胡文迪）

四、实操训练

1. 根据笔顺和规格要求,在四线三格本上练习英文字母大小写。注意执笔方法、写字姿势、规格、笔顺等情况。

2. 分别使用钢笔和粉笔反复练习以下句子:

The quick brown fox jumps over a lazy dog.

学习目标

◆ 能使用线条或几何图形等画出教学简笔画
◆ 训练重点：使用线条或几何图形画出简笔画
◆ 训练难点：根据教学内容需要创作简笔画

一、简笔画技能概述

简笔画是采用最简练的线条和最基本的平面形象描绘出物象本质特征和基本形态的图画。它富有童趣，形式简单，主旨明确，作画快捷，运用广泛，是一种功能性很强的教学手段。简笔画寥寥几笔就能表达很多信息，有助于英语教师直观教学，是教师在讲解语言知识、传递语言信息时经常运用的教学方法和手段，这种具有教学功能的简笔画称为"教学简笔画"。它应用于教学的途径主要有四种：黑板画、卡纸教具、课件插图和微课制作。

教学简笔画的设计应遵循以下三个原则。

1. 简洁性原则

教学简笔画突出一个"简"字，即用最简洁流畅的线条勾勒出事物的大概形象。如果线条过于繁琐，不但会浪费时间，更重要的是影响整堂课的教学进度和教学内容的完整性，进而影响学生的学习效果。

2. 针对性原则

设计和运用简笔画，要有针对性，要紧扣教材，突出内容主旨，能够有效地突出教学目标、内容要点,有效地突破教学的重点和难点。教师应当认真分析教学内容的难易程度、学生的理解能力等,做到有的放矢地设计和使用简笔画。

3.高效性原则

课堂教学时间有限,教师在使用简笔画进行教学时,要凝练绘画的时间,突出表达的主题。不要花费太长时间关注绘画细节,否则会失去教学简笔画的优势,不仅达不到辅助课堂教学的目的,反而会耽误教学原本的进程。这就要求教师拥有一定的分析概括能力和绘画能力,课前充分备课,构思好简笔画内容。

二、技能训练方法

(一)基本笔画练习

学会画简笔画之前先练习一些基本笔画和图形,有利于尽快掌握简笔画绘画技能。笔画练习主要有四种:线条的练习、圆的练习、方形的练习和三角形的练习。

1.线条的练习

线条是构成简笔画的最基本元素,线的把握为构成形块奠定了基础,形块间的组合又构成了物体的结构,所以在学习简笔画之初应该先练习画线。画线条要求横平竖直,在此基础上再尝试曲线、波浪线等。

2.圆的练习

圆形是很多物体的基本型,例如太阳、球类、水果等。练习种类包括正圆、半圆、椭圆和各类圆形的组合,要求完成的形状匀称饱满。开始练习时可以先用十字定点,再连接各点,熟练后要达到一笔成型。

3.方形的练习

生活中许多静物和建筑可以概括为方形。练习种类包括正方形、长方形、梯形、菱形和各类方形的组合,要求完成的形状规整完整、方正挺拔。开始练习时要求线条平直,形状规整,熟练后要达到快速、准确、完整。

4. 三角形的练习

简笔画中有许多植物、食物、文具等是三角形。练习种类包括正三角形、等边三角形、钝角三角形等各类三角形和多个不同类型三角形的组合,要求完成的形状规则整齐,线条有力。开始练习时要求线条平直,形状完整饱满,熟练后要达到快速准确。

（二）简笔画的概括归纳法

会画简笔画是用简笔画辅助英语教学的基础。画简笔画看似简单，实则需要抓住典型事物特点，具有一定概括能力和一定的绘画技能等多种能力。

运用简化、概括归纳和夸张的手法，将复杂形状进行高度概括，变成圆、方、三角等基本几何形体，然后进行相应的变形和组合，就可以画出想要的画面了。

以圆形为例，在圆形内加入线和点就可以变成篮球、橙子、甜甜圈等。

在圆形内外添加线和形，可以让圆形千变万化，造型多样，如苹果树、热气球、向日葵等。

给圆形加上不同的五官，可以变成不同的人物。

把圆形切掉一半，辅以线条可以变成公鸡、西瓜、鲸鱼等。

将圆形变扁，画成椭圆形，增加点和线可以变成鹦鹉、企鹅等。

技能训练方法视频

（济南幼儿师范高等
专科学校　乔　炜）

三、分主题绘画示例

在日常练习时可采用分主题的形式练习简笔画。如以"weather"为主题,练习"sunny,cloudy,rainy,snowy,windy"等不同天气状况的画法。

四、简笔画在教学中的应用

在不同教学环节和课型中,运用简笔画辅助教学可以帮助学生更加直观地理解所学内容,让课堂变得更加生动有趣,激发学生学习兴趣,提升教学效果。

(一)简笔画在热身导入环节中的应用

小学英语的部分话题可以以简笔画的形式导入。例如,在导入"Time"这个话题时,教师可先在黑板上画一个大圆圈,然后让学生猜测"What is it?"学生有的猜"It's a playground."有的猜"Perhaps it's a moon cake."有的猜"Maybe it's a plate."学生对猜测兴趣浓厚,给出的答案异彩纷呈。这时,教师简单几笔,在大圆上依次填上时针分针后,学生便恍然大悟道:"It's a clock."随着谜底的破解,教师自然导入对话主题"What time is it"。

教学案例视频

(练习者:郎 婕)

(二)简笔画在呈现新知环节中的应用

运用简笔画可以将生活中各种场景栩栩如生地再现,使学生犹如置身于生活之中。利用简笔画快捷、易绘的特点,针对教学的需要灵活绘制,适时控制信息量,分解教学难点,让学生一步一步扩大知识量,由浅入深地学习。

以PEP《英语(三年级起点)》三年级下册Unit 6 How many?为例。教学句型How many kites can you see? I can see...时,教师在黑板上逐步画出湖泊、小鱼、小鸟、树,树上结出苹果等景色,最后画上风筝。让学生在学习时充满期待:我们还将看到什么?在期待中学习句型,在期待中反复运用句型,从而在不知不觉中掌握语言知识。在介绍完所有内容后,还可以引导学生自由想象,在这样一个美丽的大自然里还有些什么。让学生通过小组合作,继续编写句子,拓展学生的英语思维和语用能力。

(济南泉景中学小学部 杨 溪)

（三）简笔画辅助词汇教学

以PEP《英语（三年级起点）》四年级上册Unit 5 Dinner's ready 中的Let's learn 为例。

主要教学任务：

1. 六个四会单词：rice, fish, beef, soup, noodles, vegetable

2. 口语交际：—What would you like? —I'd like some ...

T: Look, this is the menu. What would you like?（老师边画rice的简笔画边问学生，鼓励学生说出该单词，其他单词的呈现也大同小异。并引导学生回答I'd like some ...）

Ss: Rice.

T: Yes. You're so smart. Let's read together. Rice.

Ss: Rice.

T: Can I have some rice?

Ss: Sure. Here you are.

分析：本课的内容是关于食物，结合简笔画，会比较容易创设情景和吸引学生的兴趣。在黑板上，创设出在饭店点菜用餐的情景，让学生在使用新学语言时能在该特定情境下进行，激发学习兴趣，活跃课堂气氛，持续吸引学生的注意力，提高学习效率。

教学案例视频

（济南泉景中学小学部
栾　芳）

（四）简笔画辅助会话教学

简笔画可以用来呈现和操练对话。以PEP《英语（三年级起点）》四年级下册Unit 1 What time is it?中的Let's talk 为例。

本课的重点句型为：What time is it? —It's ... It's time to/for ... 词组为：get up, go to school, go home, go to bed。

在呈现 What time is it? It's 6：30. It's time to get up. 时，教师画一个表盘并标出时间 6：30，相对应画出起床的情景。用同样的方法把其他对话呈现出来，最后形成的黑板简笔画还可以在练习和输出环节中再次使用。

教学案例视频

（济南泉景中学小学部
张 琳）

（五）简笔画在时态教学中的应用

简笔画也可应用在时态教学中，特别是不同时态的比较。例如对一般将来时、现在进行时、一般过去时进行比较。The girl is going to eat an apple.（一般将来时）The girl is eating an apple.（现在进行时）The girl ate an apple.（一般过去时）

（济南泉景中学小学部　高　瞻）

（六）简笔画在故事教学中的应用

以PEP《英语（三年级起点）》五年级上册Unit 6 In a nature park 中的Story time 为例。

主要学习任务：

1. 阅读并理解故事内容，回答相应的问题。

2. 理解短文内容的层次，能够顺利朗读短文。

3. 能在记忆的基础上，复述短文的主要内容。

T:　What a nice day! Let's go to a nature park!（画一个大圈）

Look at that beautiful bridge!（画一座漂亮的桥）

There are beautiful mountains and trees.（画上山脉和树木）

...

T:　The nature park is very beautiful. I love it very much. Do you remember what's it like? Let's describe it and draw it again.

Ss:　Yes. In the nature park, there is a beautiful bridge. The mountains and trees are pretty.

...

故事学习的难点在于内容多且复杂，学生虽然可以理解，但是难于记忆或复述。借助简

笔画,教师用语言边描述文本内容,边用简笔画画出相关内容,加深学生对文本的理解。然后再解释文本,最后让学生根据简笔画内容复述故事内容,检验学生对文本的理解,培养语用能力。

教学案例视频

(济南泉景中学小学部
张 铮)

(七)简笔画辅助语音教学

简笔画辅助语音教学主要用于展示发音要领。英语中有些音素,如三个鼻音:/m/、/n/ 和 /ŋ/,发音部位指示和发音方法示范都比较困难。用简笔画区分指示舌的活动及位置、唇的张合和气流通道,就比较容易使学生掌握发音要领。

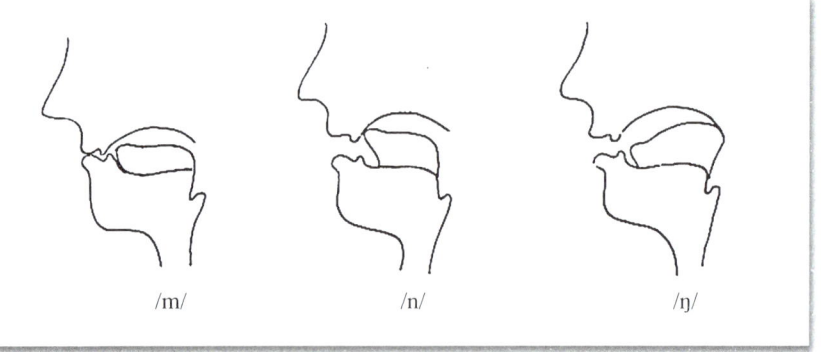

/m/ /n/ /ŋ/

(八)简笔画的其他教学辅助作用

1. 简笔画辅助课堂教学评价

课堂评价是教学中的重要环节,它能够调动学生的学习积极性,直接影响到学习效果。简笔画能够丰富评价形式,使评价更加多样有趣。例如借助简笔画进行"小猪佩奇回家"比赛,激励课上表现。

(济南泉景中学小学部　张荣荣)

2. 简笔画辅助创设情境

利用简笔画不仅有助于课文文本的教学,还能帮助创设语言学习情境。以PEP《英语(三年级起点)》三年级下册 Unit 3 At the zoo 中的 Let's talk 为例。教师用简笔画在黑板上呈现一幅动物园的景象,让学生仿佛置身于动物园,开阔了学生的想象空间,丰富了课堂内容。

(济南泉景中学小学部　李　磊)

五、实操训练

1. 用卡纸简笔画画出下列动物词汇。

monkey panda tiger bird elephant

fish horse frog sheep

bear cat pig dog duck

（济南泉景中学小学部　魏悦戎　崔　晓）

2.用黑板简笔画设计并画出PEP《英语(三年级起点)》六年级上册Unit 2 Ways to go to school中的Let's learn的词汇教学内容。

(济南泉景中学小学部　王晓玲)

模块三 | 歌曲歌谣

学习目标

◆ 能自主演唱或者跟唱英文歌曲歌谣

◆ 演唱时英语语音准确、音量适中，表情、姿态自然

◆ 掌握教唱英文歌曲的步骤、方法和手段

◆ 根据教学需要选择歌曲和进行歌曲改词

一、歌曲歌谣技能概述

歌曲歌谣易学易唱、富于童趣，深受少年儿童的喜爱。它旋律优美，节奏明快，让人身心愉悦，能够创设轻松的学习氛围；它的歌词简短，不断重复，便于记忆，符合语言学习规律。此外，英语语音、语调的训练离不开重音、节奏、速度、连读、失去爆破等知识和技能，学唱英语歌曲能自然而然地习得语言知识和技能，因此利用歌曲歌谣进行英语教学是促进语言能力发展的有效途径。

我们所需练习的英文歌曲歌谣分为两类：一是教学歌曲，指为达到某一教学目的选择的歌曲，如为练习某一音素、语法结构、某一课词汇等编写的歌曲。第二类是欣赏歌曲，其目的是提高英语学习兴趣，感受异域文化。例如，大家耳熟能详的《音乐之声》中的歌曲 "Do Re Mi"。

二、技能训练方法

歌曲歌谣技能分为学唱技能、选取技能和教唱技能。

（一）学唱技能训练

1. 学唱步骤及方法

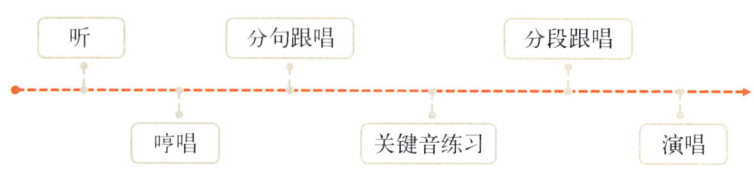

学唱英文歌曲歌谣的一般步骤是听、哼唱、分句跟唱、关键音练习、分段跟唱和演唱。听是学唱技能训练的起点。先听曲调,曲调基本掌握后再有意识地听英语语音,注意识别连读、失去爆破等情况。关键音练习时,注意拖音一般在单词的元音上,元音后的辅音在元音所属曲谱拖音的最后发出。演唱时要注意歌词的连读、失去爆破。演唱时英语发音准确、音量适中,表情姿态自然,尽量有动作。

2. 学唱注意事项

在练习演唱歌曲的同时要关注表情、姿态的训练。为了减轻个人演唱的心理负担,训练之初可采用小组的形式进行练习,小组练习时关注身势语的运用和训练。既要唱英文歌,又要加肢体语言,一开始对大家来说可能有点难度。技能练习可以由易到难,循序渐进地进行。可以先练习边拍手边唱,然后尝试手指谣,等到熟练之后再加上一定的身势语。

(二)选取技能训练

教学需要是选择歌曲歌谣的前提。选取歌曲歌谣时可以根据教学内容、教学环节、课型等有针对性地选择。

1. 教学歌曲歌谣选取步骤及方法

(1)根据教学环节选取歌曲歌谣。

在不同的教学环节,选择的歌曲歌谣是不尽相同的。在热身导入时,要选择节奏欢快、能活跃气氛的歌曲歌谣。在呈现和机械性练习阶段,以重复歌词较多的chant为主。在有意义和交际性练习阶段,可以选择配合动作的歌曲歌谣以达到巩固提高的目的。

(2)根据教学内容选取歌曲歌谣。

教材分析是选取歌曲歌谣的基础。对教材的分析大致包括对语言知识点和文化知识点的分析。之后,搜索、选择歌词符合教学内容的歌曲。如果有现成的歌曲歌谣,可以直接使用。在很多情况下,歌曲歌谣中的歌词与所需练习的目标内容并不十分契合,需要进行歌曲改词。歌曲改词一般方法为旧曲换新词和替换部分歌词。旧曲换新词要求新词同旧词结构和音节上应基本相同。只替换部分歌词,例如在歌曲"Muffin Man"中"Do you know the Muffin Man, the Muffin Man, the Muffin Man",将"Muffin Man"替换为"Police Man"。

2. 教学歌曲歌谣选取注意事项

如果没有合适的视频资源,播放歌曲歌谣时可以辅以PPT展示图片,帮助学生理解教学内容,提高歌曲歌谣应用效果。

（三）教唱技能训练

1. 教唱步骤及方法

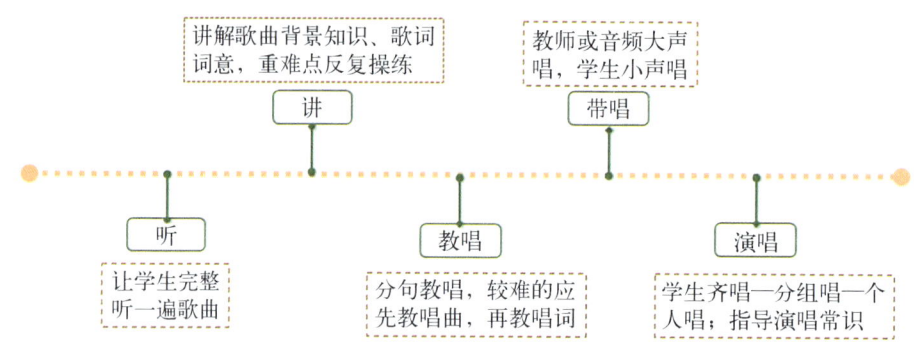

教唱英文歌曲歌谣的一般步骤是听、讲、教唱、带唱、演唱。先让学生完整听一遍，整体感知歌曲；然后讲解歌曲文化背景知识、歌词词意，着重讲解发音重难点并反复操练；接着分句教唱，较难的可以先唱曲，再教唱词；然后学生跟随教师或者音频小声唱，最后学生通过齐唱、分组唱、个人唱等形式进行演唱练习。教师在此过程中注意指导表情、手势动作等演唱常识。

以歌曲"Muffin Man"为例，教唱可以分为四个步骤：

步骤1：感知歌曲

播放歌曲、展示歌词。歌曲歌词的展示尽量采用多模态的形式，多使用视频、图片、实物等。

步骤2：讲解

讲解背景文化知识，包括什么是Muffin；Muffin与cupcake的异同；拓展词汇Baker以及Drury Lane。

讲解语音知识，包括易错音Man和Lane中字母a的不同发音，以及连读lives on /lɪvzɒn/的发音方法。

步骤3：教唱和带唱

可以利用媒体资源多次教唱，逐句带唱。注意易错音和连读的练习。

步骤4：练唱

采用多种形式组织练唱，避免单一形式引起枯燥乏味的感觉。例如，全班练唱、半班练唱、小组练唱、男女生分别唱等。教师也可以使用不同的乐器或者发声教具组织练唱，让学生持续保持练唱的新鲜感。

2. 教唱注意事项

歌曲歌谣是教学的辅助形式。由于运用歌曲的教学目的不同和学生的个体差异，教唱时不必要求每位学生每一句都唱得优美动听，只要能够达到运用歌曲实现教学目标的目的即可。

三、分类型歌曲歌谣示例

在日常练习时可采用分类型练习歌曲歌谣的形式。

1. 拍手歌谣

案例视频

（练习者：吴珊珊）

2. 手指谣

案例视频

（练习者：邴　婕）

3. 简单动作歌谣

案例视频

（练习者：杨　柳）

4. 复杂动作歌谣

案例视频

（练习者：陈欣然）

四、歌曲歌谣在教学中的应用

在不同教学环节和课型中，运用歌曲歌谣辅助教学可以让课堂变得更加生动有趣，激发学生学习兴趣，提升教学效果。

（一）歌曲歌谣在热身导入环节中的应用

在导入"community"这个主题时，教师使用了自编歌曲。自编歌曲内容有关"What's my name? What do I do? Where do I live?"在师生问答间引出了本课主题。接着通过问题"What do you often do in the community?"与学生进一步讨论共同生活的社区，加深学生对社区概念的了解。最后通过问题"Who makes our community such a good place?"导入文本内容。

（二）歌曲歌谣在练习环节中的应用

这段歌谣在新授课 Do you like pears?的最后阶段，在学生对基本句型有了一定的掌握后，通过反复呈现 Do you like ...? 及其答语进行总结和巩固，一方面练习了本课时的主要句型，另一方面也为下一阶段的模音与拓展练习奠定了语言基础。

（三）歌曲歌谣辅助语音教学

以 PEP《英语（三年级起点）》三年级下册 unit 3 At the zoo 中的 Let's spell 为例，学生通过跟唱表演字母歌复习学过的 26 个字母及字母发音。

案例视频

（济南市市中区育秀小学
田　静）

案例视频

（济南泉景中学小学部
张　铮）

案例视频

（济南市市中区育秀小学
周淑娟）

（四）歌曲歌谣辅助词汇教学

利用学生们熟悉的歌曲进行词汇操练是词汇教学的常见教学活动。以歌曲"Bingo"为例，将所学词汇tiger, panda, sheep, horse放到歌曲中，替换词汇Bingo，在反复的歌唱中进行有意义的操练。

案例视频

（练习者：张瑶瑶、
翟宁宁）

五、实操训练

1. 学唱歌曲"Twinkle Twinkle Little Star"并配以简单动作。

2. 依照文中的教唱步骤，选择恰当的教学资源并制作课件，练习教唱歌曲"Muffin Man"。

3. 选择小学英语教材中的一课，运用歌曲歌谣进行教学。

专题四

教师资格证考试
模拟训练

◆ 了解教师资格证考试面试的流程
◆ 知道必答题环节和答辩环节的区别
◆ 根据样题进行教学设计并答辩

一、面试概述

教师资格证考试分为笔试和面试两部分,其中面试主要是对申请教师资格人员应具备的教师基本素养(职业认知、心理素质、仪表仪态、言语表达、思维品质等)、职业发展潜质和教育教学实践能力的考察。面试采取结构化面试、情景模拟等方式,通过抽题备课(教学设计)、回答规定问题、试讲(演示教学设计或模拟讲课)、答辩、评分等环节进行。

1. 面试时间

20分钟:主观提问5分钟+试讲10分钟(独立严格计时)+提问5分钟

2. 面试流程

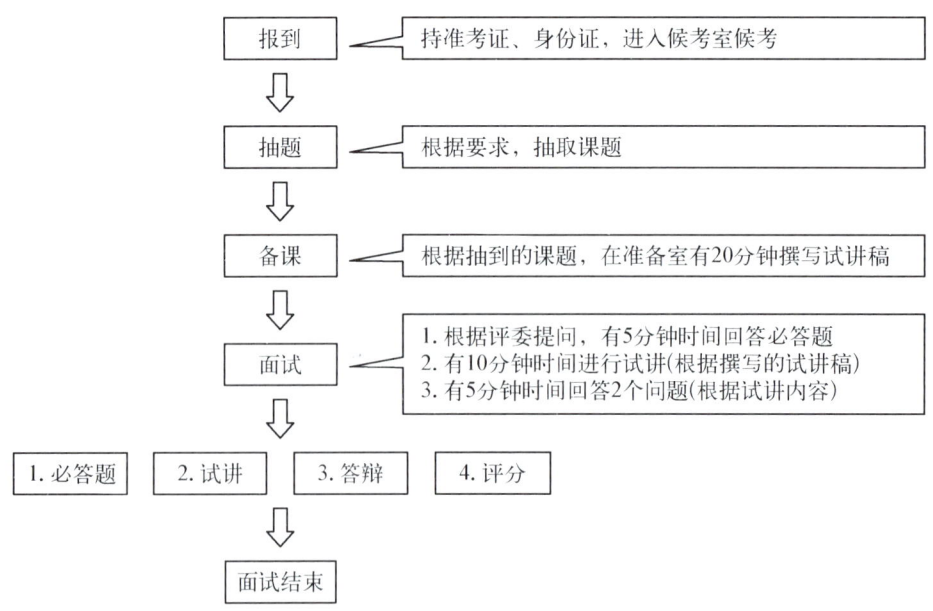

3. 面试过程细节解析

- 考生上报信息。(尊敬的各位考官您好,我是＊号考生)
- 宣读导语。(主考官:同学,你好! 欢迎参加面试。本次面试共20分钟,程序如下:先请你回答两个规定问题,然后试讲(展示)。下面我们随机抽取两个问题,请你认真听清题目思考后回答,共5分钟,注意把握时间。好,请听题)
- 考生答题。(回答完后,要说"回答完毕,下面开始我的试讲")
- 考生试讲。
- 考生答辩。(考官会宣读:下面根据试讲的内容提问两个问题,请你认真听清题目思考后回答,共5分钟,注意把握时间。好。请听题)
- 提交材料。(面试结束后,考生提交试题、备课纸和面试顺序号,领取准考证后离场。注意,备课纸也是评分依据材料)

二、必答题及样题

必答题内容类型大致包括自我认知类、沟通协调类、应急应变类、计划组织类、综合分析类等,重点考察申请人的教师观、学生观、家校合作、教学问题处理、教育时政等方面的内容。

1. 习总书记提出教师不但要教书更要育人,你怎么看?
2. 你觉得自己适合当老师吗? 为什么?
3. 如何评价一个学生?
4. 小明上你课的时候,常常不听课,作为任课教师你怎么办?
5. 小明的作业常常不完成,你与他的家长联系,他的家长认为这事不重要,你怎么办?
6. 学生成绩下降厉害,其家长向你求助,你作为班主任,怎么办?
7. 走进教室,你发现黑板上有一幅漫画,旁边写着你的名字,你怎么办?
8. 小明的考试成绩不理想,他伤心地哭了,作为教师的你会怎么办?
9. 对于性格孤僻、胆小、不爱说话的孩子,教师如何处理?
10. 学生上课搞怪动作,你怎么办?
11. 下课好一会了,老师还在讲课,一个学生说早该下课了,老师气呼呼地说你们下课吧,拂袖而去,你怎么看?
12. 老师让学生讲自己的感受和经历,以此引出教学内容,你怎么看?
13. 学生由于父母离异,远离同学的交往圈子,喜欢独来独往,不愿意参加集体活动。你将怎样帮助他?
14. 学生早恋怎么办?
15. 博士当中小学老师,大材小用,你怎么看?

三、答辩问题解析及样题

◇ 答辩问题解析

1. 你确定的教学目标是什么? 围绕教学目标开展了哪些教学活动?

答题要点:

(1)根据本节课的教学内容和该年级的学生情况确定的目标分别是……其中,知识目

标……技能目标……过程与方法目标……情感态度与价值观……文化目标……

（2）围绕教学目标开展了以下几项活动：

在新授阶段，我设计了……通过这些活动落实……的目标；在练习环节，我设计了……通过这些活动落实……的目标；在巩固环节我设计了……通过这些活动落实……的目标；在拓展环节我设计了……通过这些活动落实……的目标。

2. 你确定的教学重难点是什么？是如何突破难点的？

答题要点：通过对教学文本分析、结合学生的学情，本节课的教学重点是……，难点是……。为有效突破教学重难点，我在教学新授环节创设……情景，采用……教学方法，设计了……活动，让学生得到有效的语言输入。在练习拓展环节，我设计了……任务，在具体的任务中，让学生运用了……知识，形成了……能力，落实教学重难点。

◇ 答辩样题

1. 在本节课中，你是如何培养学生英语学习兴趣的？

2. 导入环节你设计了哪些活动？这样设计有什么作用？

3. 在练习环节，你都设计了哪些活动？为什么这样设计？

4. 本节课你采用了哪些教学策略和教学方法？

5. 在课堂上你是怎样组织学生进行合作学习的？

6. 在本节课中，你是如何引导学生进行对话的？

7. 哪个环节体现出了学生的独立思考？

8. 你试讲中的优点和不足是什么？

9. 本节课中哪些环节体现了哪些学科核心素养？

10. 通过这节课，学生哪些方面能力得到提升？

四、面试模拟样题（试讲）

模拟样题（人教版）

样题 1　某某考生教师资格面试题　　　抽题时间 10：20

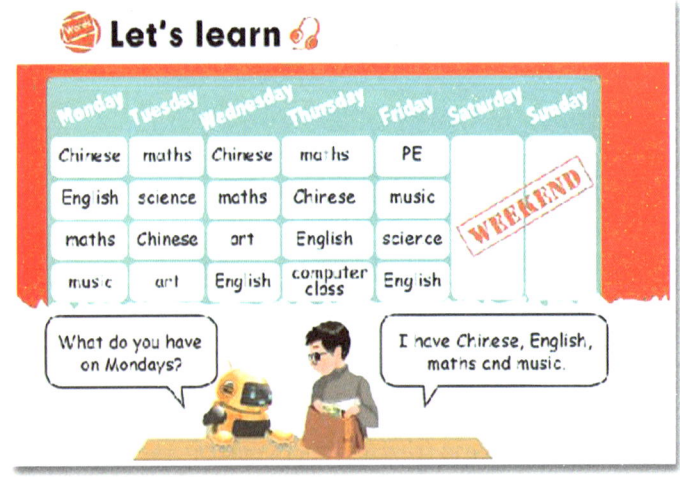

要求：1.教师用全英进行试讲。

2.教师要有示范性朗读。

3.教师的所讲内容教学目标明确，重难点突出，练习有梯度。

样题2 某某考生教师资格面试题　　　抽题时间10：20

要求：1.教师用全英进行试讲。

2.教师要有示范性朗读。

3.教师的所讲内容教学目标明确，重难点突出，练习有梯度。

样题3 某某考生教师资格面试题　　　抽题时间10：20

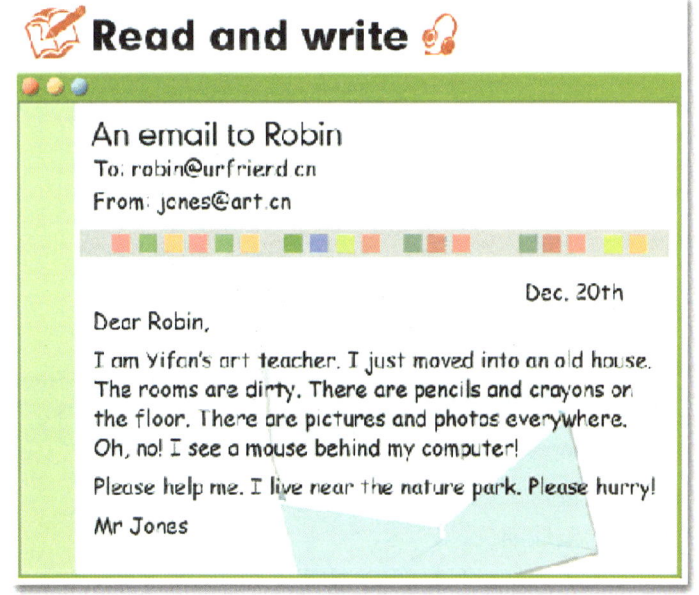

要求：1. 教师用全英进行试讲。

　　　2. 教师要有示范性朗读。

　　　3. 教师的所讲内容教学目标明确,重难点突出,练习有梯度。

样题4　某某考生教师资格面试题　　　　抽题时间10∶20

要求：1. 教师用全英进行试讲。

　　　2. 教师要有示范性朗读。

　　　3. 教师的所讲内容教学目标明确,重难点突出,练习有梯度。

模拟样题(外研版)

样题1　某某考生教师资格面试题　　　　抽题时间10∶20

要求：1. 教师用全英进行试讲。

　　　2. 教师要有示范性朗读。

　　　3. 教师的所讲内容教学目标明确,重难点突出,练习有梯度。

样题2　某某考生教师资格面试题　　　抽题时间10：20

要求：1. 教师用全英进行试讲。

2. 教师要有示范性朗读。

3. 教师的所讲内容教学目标明确,重难点突出,练习有梯度。

样题3　某某考生教师资格面试题　　　抽题时间10：20

要求：1. 教师用全英进行试讲。

2. 教师要有示范性朗读。

3. 教师的所讲内容教学目标明确,重难点突出,练习有梯度。

样题 4　某某考生教师资格面试题　　　抽题时间 10 : 20

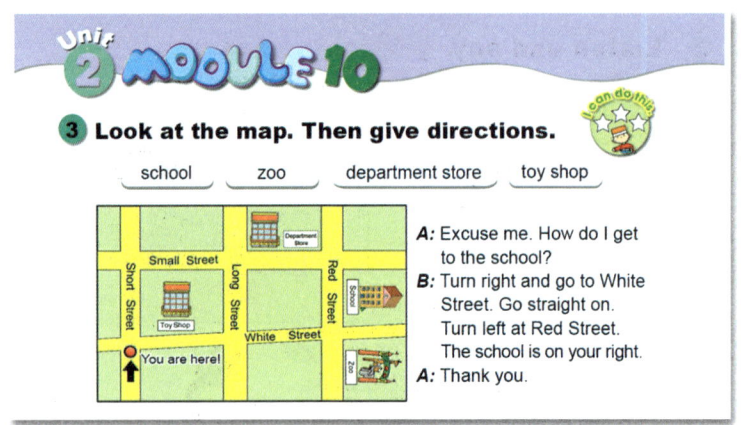

要求：1. 教师用全英进行试讲。

　　　2. 教师要有示范性朗读。

　　　3. 教师的所讲内容教学目标明确，重难点突出，练习有梯度。

模拟样题（牛津版）

样题 1　某某考生教师资格面试题

　　　　　抽题时间 10 : 20

要求：1. 教师用全英进行试讲。

　　　2. 教师要有示范性朗读。

　　　3. 教师的所讲内容教学目标明确，

　　　　重难点突出，练习有梯度。

样题2　某某考生教师资格面试题
　　　　抽题时间10：20
要求：1. 教师用全英进行试讲。
　　　2. 教师要有示范性朗读。
　　　3. 教师的所讲内容教学目标明确，
　　　　 重难点突出，练习有梯度。

样题3　某某考生教师资格面试题
　　　　抽题时间10：20
要求：1. 教师用全英进行试讲。
　　　2. 教师要有示范性朗读。
　　　3. 教师的所讲内容教学目标明确，
　　　　 重难点突出，练习有梯度。

Say and act

Let's join the club!

Peter and Danny are talking with Alice in the classroom.

Peter & Danny: Hello, Alice.
Alice: Hi, Peter and Danny.
Danny: There's a badminton club in our school. Peter and I want to join it. Would you like to come with us?
Alice: Oh, sure. I'd love to.
Peter: Will Kitty come too? Does she like playing badminton?
Alice: No, she doesn't. She never plays badminton. She likes playing volleyball, basketball and table tennis.

样题4　某某考生教师资格面试题
　　　　抽题时间 10：20
要求：1. 教师用全英进行试讲。
　　　2. 教师要有示范性朗读。
　　　3. 教师的所讲内容教学目标明确，
　　　　 重难点突出，练习有梯度。

学习目标

- 了解试讲的流程
- 能够在规定时间内完成教学设计
- 能够根据不同课型在规定时间内完成模拟讲课

一、试讲概述

1. 什么是"试讲"

试讲，又叫模拟讲课。它是一种在模拟课堂的情景下开展的教学活动。教师根据事先设计好的教案，在没有学生的情况下上课，完整地呈现所有的教学流程，模拟过程中有提问、有引导、有启发、有评价。在模拟课堂过程中，各个环节要缩短生生互动、师生互动及学生展示的时间，仅以模拟形式进行，是一种有预设而无实际生成的"模拟课堂"教学。"小学英语模拟讲课"则是模拟小学英语课堂，对象是小学生，课堂上要完全运用英语来授课的模拟教学。

2. "小学英语模拟讲课"的注意事项

（1）时间。

"lead-in（导入）"的设计一定要有趣，符合学生的特点，在整个presentation部分占用的时间不能过长，导入要熟练，表达要流畅。在对学生提问问题时，一定要模拟真实的英语课堂，给学生留出合适的时间来思考和启发，虽然没有学生，但是依然要当作有学生来认真讲课。模拟讲课的时间有限，但是非常有必要留出几秒的时间来让学生思考。

（2）内容。

不要因为是"模拟讲课"，没有学生就过于随意地设计不符合实际的、大而空的教学环节，这样只能失去"模拟讲课"的意义。"模拟讲课"一定要呈现清楚的教学环节，各个环节要一步一步过渡，要有清楚的衔接语与过渡语。同时，在"小学英语模拟讲课"设计中要有多样的、吸引学生兴趣的教学方法以及练习形式，例如：个人（individual work）、搭档（pair work）、小组合作（group work）等多种练习形式，虽然是"无学生"，但是适合学生的练习形式一定不可缺少。

（3）情感。

课堂上虽然无"生"，但是眼中要有"生"。在设计教案时，一定要符合小学生的特点，同时要依据他们不同年级的学情来设计出适合他们的教案。例如：小学生活泼好动，喜欢夸张、有趣、吸引人的学习方式，所以在 Warm up 和 Presentation 环节，我们可以充分利用歌曲（song）、视频（video）、歌谣（chant）、图片（picture）、谜语（riddle）、自由谈话（free talk）、肢体动作（body language）等不同的形式来吸引学生的兴趣，为模拟讲课以及有效的模拟生成打下良好的基础。在教学过程中也要跟随自己的教学肢体语言（body language），进行必要的微笑、点头等，不要总是盯着书本或黑板，或者不敢抬头往前看，让人一看就没有激情，没有自信。

（4）区别。

一定要准确区分"模拟讲课"与"说课"。"模拟讲课"是在规定的时间内详细地讲出教学内容，没有必要明确地指出教学目标、教学重难点等，重点是如何上课；而"说课"则是要说明白所讲的教材、教学目标、教学重难点、教学方法、教学过程、板书等各方面内容是什么。有时候，说课也侧重于说教学过程，其他部分可以少说，但是不可缺少的组成部分。

（5）技巧。

有的"模拟讲课"规定是不需要带任何东西的，但是有的允许带相关的PPT、图片或者小教具。PPT制作不要太复杂，因为时间有限，要让听课的人能在短时间之内捕捉到本课的重点内容，相反，过于复杂的PPT会让讲课的人跟着PPT走，容易乱了阵脚，影响上课的效果。相关的图片或者奖励学生的物品，如：小贴画等小教具，如果运用得恰到好处，会起到事半功倍的效果。另外，模拟讲课的细节不可忽视。从走进教室，教师就需要注意一举一动，从一个甜美的微笑到大方、自然的教态，优美、流畅的英语语音语调，再加上工整、美观、重点突出的板书、清晰、明确的教学环节设计等，肯定能吸引学生的注意力，取得模拟讲课的成功。

综上所述，只有了解了"小学英语模拟讲课"的含义、特点以及其注意事项，才能设计出符合学生特点，学情以及富有小学英语学科特色的教学设计，再加上自己的精彩"演绎"，肯定能达到意想不到的课堂效果。

二、试讲流程及解析

1. 抽题

某某考生教师资格面试试题

抽题时间：8:10

要求：1. 教师用全英进行试讲。

2. 教师要有示范性朗读。

3. 教师的所讲内容教学目标明确，重难点突出，练习有梯度。

2. 准备

（备考室）撰写试讲稿。

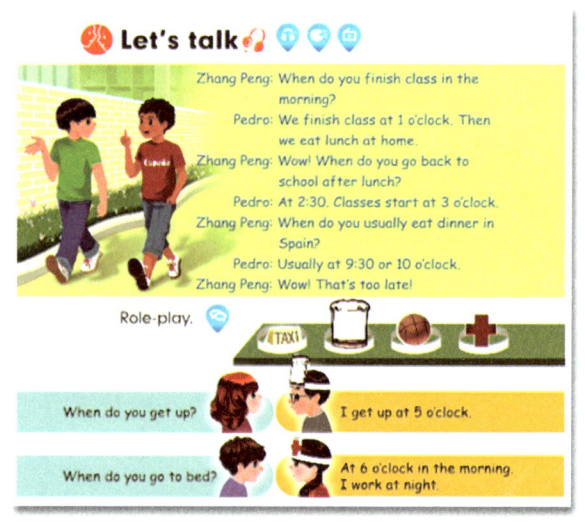

3. 试讲

注：试讲内容选自PEP《英语(三年级起点)》五年级下册Unit 1 My day中的Let's talk课时教学设计。

环节	试讲内容	动作	备注
敲门		一般情况下敲三声门后进入试讲室,鞠躬表示礼貌后开始问候	
问候	Good morning/afternoon, my dear judges. I am number _____ candidate, applying for primary English teacher. My topic is _____. May I begin? Thank you.	问候时要与考官评委们进行眼神交流,面带微笑	在说到 My topic is _____. 时,要立即回身在黑板上写下课题名称。书写时注意:1. 书写准确,单词拼写、笔画和笔顺不能有错误;2. 课题板书要居中,不能上挑或是下偏
试讲	Step 1. Warm up Hello, children. Nice to meet you. I'm your guest teacher. Do you want to know something about me? Let's listen to a rap. Step 2. Presentation 1. Lead-in. What time is it? It's ... Look! We start our English class at ... 2. Listen and answer the questions. (1) Let's know a new friend—Pedro. What are they talking about? Listen and answer the questions. Question 1: Where are Zhang Peng and Pedro? Question 2: Where is Pedro from? (2) Watch a video clip about Spain. T: Do you know Spain? Let's enjoy a video about Spain. 3. Watch the video. (Let's talk) (1) T: Do you know Pedro's life in Spain? Let's watch the video and answer the question: When does Pedro finish class in the morning? (2) Here "finish" means stop. "Finish class" means the class is over. Read after me, please.	此处可以示范演唱rap的一小段,注意演唱时配合一定的肢体动作或者简单拍手打拍子 此处要做好动作,假装手中有clock,向学生展示,互动交流 此处可以用动作,用手指课件,示意评委此处会有课件辅助教学 用手示意评委此处观看视频,并做好师生互动环节	(时间约为1分钟) 面对空桌子,要做到眼中有学生,此环节要有面部表情和眼神交流 (时间约为4分钟) 问题抛出后,给学生们留存3—5秒钟,接着提问学生,并做好学生回答的评价 此处增加学生练习提问,教师做好评价 此处要体现出学生的跟读练习和教师评价

（续表）

环节	试 讲 内 容	动 作	备 注
试讲	(3) Practice in pairs. When do you _____? We _____ at _____. 4. Read and underline. (1) Do you know Pedro's other activities? Read the text and underline them. (2) "Start class" means … Can you guess "Go back to school"? … (3) Work in groups and circle Pedro's time, and read them aloud. Step 3. Practice 1. Listen and repeat. Listen and repeat. Pay attention to your pronunciation and intonation. 2. Fill in the blanks and play the roles in pairs. 3. Sing a song "Pedro's Day". Step 4. Production 1. Match and show. Match the time with the pictures and share in your group. Step 5. Homework Choose one of the tasks to finish. 1. Draw a picture of your timetable and mark the time. 2. To be a reporter and interview your parents' timetable.	此处试讲时，教师要走到学生展示的位置，眼神与展示的学生进行交流 教师要走到学生小组中间进行指导 此处可以示范演唱"Pedro's Day"的一小段，注意演唱时配合一定的肢体动作或者简单拍手打拍子 在小组交流展示过程中，教师要适时地提问学生问题，意在引导学生说出"清洁工很辛苦，她的付出换来城市的洁净，我们要保持卫生，尊重清洁工" 试讲时，可以利用板书设计或是课件突出主题，让评委明白考生对德育目标的落实	展示要用小组形式，让评委听明白，每小组展示完毕后做好评价 此处试讲时要突出问题提问后，经过学生独立自主的学习后才个人展示，然后教师评价 展示环节，要示意学生到教师前面展示，学生展示完成后教师可以自己选择一个点进行重点强调并做整体评价 （时间约为2分钟） 试讲时要注意教师的指令语，让评委听明白，听的过程要求学生注意语音、语调并模音 试讲时注意，在任务布置之后，要有展示和反馈评价 （时间约为2分钟） 在学生展示过程中引导学生建立感恩思想 Different time but the same work! Different jobs but the same contributions! （时间控制在1分钟内） 试讲时，要说清楚作业的分层设计和可选择性
结束	Class is over. Thank you for your listening.	面带微笑，说完结束语，要鞠躬表示感谢	擦黑板

164

三、试讲模板及样例

（一）模板

✧　模板一（词汇、对话、语音、语法课型）

Teaching Objectives	
Key Points	
Difficult Points	
Teaching Methods	
Teaching Aids	
Teaching Procedures	Step 1　Warm up and lead-in Step 2　Presentation Step 3　Practice Step 4　Production Homework Blackboard Design

✧　模板二（阅读课型、听力练习）

Teaching Objectives	
Key Points	
Difficult Points	
Teaching Methods	
Teaching Aids	
Teaching Procedures	Step 1　Warm up and lead-in Step 2　Pre-reading/listening Step 3　While-reading/listening 　　　　Task 1　Fast reading/listening 　　　　Task 2　Careful reading/listening Step 4　Post-reading/listening Step 5　Summary Homework Blackboard Design

（二）试讲样例

【教学内容】

PEP《英语（三年级起点）》六年级上册 Unit 2 Ways to go to school 中的 Let's learn

I. Warm-up

1. Free talk.

Hello, children. Nice to meet you. I'm your guest teacher. Do you want to know something about me? Let me tell you. My name is Daisy. I am an English teacher. I like playing sports. I often go to work on foot. Do you know "on foot"? Look here, please! "On foot" means walk. I go to the supermarket on foot. I go to the park on foot. I go to the bookstore on foot. I go to work on foot. Can you ask me: "How do I go to work?" Who can try? You, please? Good! "How do you go to work?" The boy, please? Good! I go to work on foot. Can you try it again? Wonderful ...

2. I am a teacher. I go to school on foot. You are students. How do you go to school? You go to work by car, by bike or by bus? Follow me "by bus", "by bus", "by bus" ... (边制作思维导图边介绍) How do you go to school? Good. Can you try it again? Wonderful! Let's practice one by one. One asks, one answers. You two, please. Very good.

3. Pair work.

Let's do a pair work. One student asks and one student answers. Let's begin. You did a good job.

4. Sing a song.

Let's sing a song. Stand up, please. "How do you come to school?"

II. Presentation & practice

1. Mrs. Smith is going to take her children to the nature park. Listen and answer. How do they get there? Do they get there by bus, by car or by taxi? Look! This is a taxi. Taxi ... Let's read it one by one. Very good! "by taxi", "by taxi". (板书呈现 by taxi) Let's listen and answer. Who can tell me the answer, the boy? Good, by bus. This time, let's listen and imitate. Now, let's have

a role play. Your group, please?

2. Today I will introduce a friend to you. Look! Who is she? She is Ann. We will meet Ann's family. Here is a passage for you. Please listen and answer "How do Ann's family go to school/ go to work/...?" Now let's listen. Yes, they have different ways. How does Ann go to school? Let's listen.

3. (依次出示Ann、dad、mum、grandparents的介绍图片) Children, we know we have different ways. Yes? (再次出示Ann图片并听录音) How does Ann go to school? Can you tell me? Good. On foot. Now let's read together. Good. Can you read? Wonderful! Now this time, let's listen again and imitate. Children, can you be Ann? Yes, the boy. Wonderful! And the lovely girl. Good try! You did a good job.

(出示图片) Ann's dad works in a bank. How does he go to work? Now, let's listen and fill. Ok? Ok, now, who can tell me? Yes, the boy. Good. I go to work by subway. (出示地铁图片) Look, this is the subway. Follow me. Subway. Subway. Yes, boys, please read it. Good. And the girls? Wonderful! We can go by subway.

Children, this time let's listen again and imitate. Now, who can be Ann's dad? Yes, all the boys have a try, ok? Good! You have done a good job! Now, children, let me tell you something about subway.

(教师读PPT内容) The subway is in underground. The first subway in China was built in Beijing in 1969. Now, subway is one of the most important transportation in many cities. It makes our life more and more convenient.

We all know Ann's dad goes to school by subway. How about her mother? Can you guess? Yes, who can try? Good guess! And you please. Now, let's listen. Look, I go to work by car. Sometimes I go to work by taxi. Look. Taxi is coming. There are many kinds of taxis. Taxi. Taxi. Yes, the yellow taxi. Now let's listen. Who can be Ann's mum? First, all the girls, please try. Wonderful! Next, who can try? The lovely boy. Ok, very good.

Ann's grandparents like traveling. Listen and choose. How do they go travelling? Now we can ask grandpa and grandma. How do you go travelling? Ok, who can give me the answers? What are the right answers? Yes, the girl, yes ABE. Yes, you are right.

Now let's fill in the blanks. We often go travelling by train, sometimes we go by ship or by plane. Yes, very good. This is a ship. Follow me, ship ship, ship ship. Now, boys. Please read it. Good! And all the girls, good! Look, it is a ship. (出示不同的ship图片) Different kinds of ships. Is it a ship? No, it is a plane. Follow me, plane, plane, plane. Can you try? Good! This group, please read it. One two go. Good. Look, they are planes. Is it a plane? No, it's a train. Follow me, train train, train train. Let's read it one by one. Good! Now there are many kinds of trains. Look, this is the bullet train. And this is the high-speed train. And the maglev train. They are all very fast.

This time, who can be Ann's grandpa and grandma? Ok, the girl, you please, very good. Have a try. Yes. Bingo! Good job!

（出示Ann一家人出行方式的表格）Now children, let's have a summary. How do you go to school/go to work/go travelling? You can use "I go ..." blabla. Look, how about Ann? Good! Dad? Yes. Mum? Wonderful! Grandpa and grandma? Yes. Who can be Ann? And say the way to go to school. Yes, you please. I go to school by bus. Bingo! Who can be Dad? The boy. Good! And mum? Yes. Wonderful! Grandpa and grandma? Yes. Excellent!

Now children, if you go travelling, how do you get there? Look! （出示三幅地图）How do you get to Dalian from Yantai? Ok, you can go by ship. How do you get to Shanghai from Beijing? You can try ... Yes. By train. What else? You can also go there by plane. How do you get to Seoul from Jinan? It's very far. You can go there by ...? Bingo. You can go there by plane. Good job!

III. Production

Now, children, you know, autumn is a beautiful season. Simon and Daming want to go travelling. Listen and underline. How do they go traveling? How do they get there? Yes, the boy. They can go there by No. 88 bus. What else? Good! By bike and by train. Children, let's read it again and do a match. Yes. You are all right.

In this part, we can see where they go/how they go/and whom with. If you want to write your travel plan, you can use them.

Please write your travel plan according to the key points. There are many ways to go somewhere. How about in the future? Please enjoy a video. The transportation are very fast now. They are very important in our daily life. They make our life more amazing and more easily. We can use less time. More and more people are yearning for the outside. The convenient transportation makes our world a big family.

IV. Homework

The homework today is:

1. Talk about your ways to go somewhere.

2. Read picture books about transportation.

四、试讲训练模拟题

参见面试模拟样题（试讲）。

模块三 说 课

学习目标

◆ 了解说课的流程
◆ 知道说课与试讲的异同
◆ 能够根据不同课型在规定时间内完成说课

一、说课概述

1. 什么是"说课"

说课，就是教师对一定的教学内容进行教学设计之后，通过口头表达的方式，对课时内容教学设计及其理论依据进行详细阐述。具体来讲就是执教者将自己的备课设计及设计理论依据说给同行或者专业人员听。在教师招考等面试环节中，就是考生将自己抽取内容的教学设计及理论依据说给评委听，其重点就是说明怎么教，为什么这样教。

2. "小学英语说课"的注意事项

目前教师资格证面试环节是采用试讲的形式，而非说课。但是在许多地区的教资招考中依然采用说课的形式来考查申请人员的教育教学实践能力。在说课时除了所有学科共有的注意事项之外，针对小学英语这一学科说课，还应多关注以下几个方面。

（1）语言。

小学英语学科说课使用的语言有中文和英文两种。至于具体使用哪一种语言，根据招考单位要求来选择。如果没有指定语言，从全局考虑建议使用中英结合的方式。当然，如果申请人英语语言运用水平好，能够在较短时间完成内容完整、思路清晰的教学设计，能够教学内容与教学语言兼顾，使用全英文说课效果会更好。使用中英结合的方式说课时，在保证语言使用正确的前提下尽可能多地使用英语。如，教学环节的一般流程用语、教学活动常见设计意图的英语表述等，是在任何课型都会用到的语言，这类语言要使用英语。

（2）动作。

适当的肢体动作有助于提高说课效果。考虑到小学英语教学对象的特点，在小学英语教学中常使用TPR教学和直观教学。在说课时，可以适时的增加肢体动作以体现这些教学理念。如在教授play soccer等运动的词汇时；在示范发音时可使用手指示范口型的大小，如

169

食指和中指并拢放在嘴前示范 /æ/ 发音时口型的大小；在热身、练习等环节可以带领学生一起做手指操等。

（3）板书。

说课过程中要边说课边完成板书，在说课结束之时形成一份优质的板书也有助于提高说课效果。除了布局合理、内容精练、板面美观等要求之外，小学英语板书还要注意书写的规范。板书字母时笔画、笔顺正确；板书单词和句子时不连笔。根据教学内容适时增加简笔画，以增添教学的多样性，展示自身才艺。

（4）唱歌。

歌曲歌谣是小学生喜爱的教学方式，也是小学英语课堂常见的教学形式。在说课时，适时的示范演唱一段歌曲歌谣能够活跃气氛、展现个人素养、体现教学理念，一举多得。如在学习完表示身体的词汇时，教师可以带领学生一边唱 "Head shoulders knees and toes" 一边做动作来巩固所学。在日常练习时大家可以挑选一些节奏欢快、旋律简单、歌词易换的歌曲有意识地练习。

二、说课流程及解析

1. 说课流程图

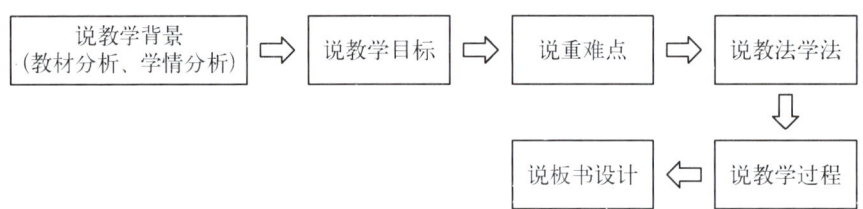

2. 说课内容及案例解析

（1）说教学背景分析。

教学背景分析主要包括教材分析和学情分析。教材分析是对教材内容的话题分析、年级内容分析、单元内容分析及课时位置分析等；学情分析从已有知识、已有技能、性格特点、发展需求等方面入手。在教学背景分析的基础之上确定教学目标及教学重难点。简言之，通过教材背景分析，让听众了解你将要说课的内容和学生情况，明确教学目标、重难点确定的依据。例如：

本节课内容是 PEP 五上 Unit 3 What would you like? 中的 Let's talk，课文话题为饮食，本节课主要围绕询问对饮食的偏好来展开教学活动，要求学生能运用句型 "What would you like to eat/to drink?" 询问别人想要吃什么喝什么，并能用 "I'd like ..." 作答。本话题内容和功能是小学英语日常交际的重要组成部分，在整个小学英语体系中是必不可少的。本课中的部分词汇 "hungry, water ..." 在三四年级中出现过，部分同学可能遗忘，所以在本节课中，此部分内容会复习。通过 Sarah 一家用餐场景的创设，引导学生理解新词汇 sandwich, drink 和 thirsty 的意思，并能够正确发音。本课的内容注重听说训练，培养学生正确的语音、语调和语感，使学生能够进行交流，并能达到灵活运用。同时为 Let's learn 的学习奠定了基础，起到了承上启下的作用。

（2）说目标。

分别叙述教学目标，注意语言表述，要选择具体的行为动词，以便教师测评和学生自评。例如：

知识目标：理解对话大意，知道句型 What would you like? I'd like... 和词汇 sandwich，drink 和 thirsty 的意思。

能力目标：能够按照正确的意群及语音、语调朗读对话，并能够进行角色表演；能够在情景中运用句型 What would you like to eat/drink? I'd like ... 询问并回答自己想要吃什么、喝什么；能够在语境中理解新单词 sandwich, drink 和 thirsty 的意思，并能够正确发音。

情感目标：养成健康的饮食习惯。了解中西方饮食文化差异，如：餐具、餐桌礼仪、饮食差异等。

（3）说重难点。

一般说来，教学重难点来源于教学目标。教学重点是学生要掌握的核心知识与技能。教学难点是学生不易掌握的知识与技能。教学重点不一定是教学难点，也有一些内容既是教学难点，又是教学重点。在教学设计时要注意分散重点，突破难点。

教学重点：学生能够在情境中运用句型 What would you like to eat? What would you like to drink? I'd like ... 并能分角色表演对话。

教学难点：学生能够在实际生活情境中用本课重点句型询问并回答某人想要吃/喝什么。

为突破重难点，我设计了以下方案：

热身环节，利用头脑风暴的形式复习所学食物类单词。根据课堂自然交流情境及情境的推进，自然导入本课主题。直接利用 Sarah 一家的场景呈现本课对话内容，教师通过问题引导、制作表格、表演对话等形式练习本课主要内容。同时设置 Chain Game 游戏，让学生们在游戏中自然而然理解、使用所学内容。利用任务型教学法，设计调查表格，从听、说过渡到读、写的活动，依据学生不同的需求，由浅入深，逐层递进，设计的任务型活动帮助学生进一步内化本课重点知识，逐步达到灵活运用本课重点知识。

（4）说教法学法。

说教法学法，就是根据说教材板块的内容阐释，在教学过程中，执教者将采用什么样的教学方法进行教学，学生在学习过程中，将使用什么样的学习方法进行有效学习。在说课的过程中，不仅仅是说明使用什么样的教学方法和学习方法，还要说明选择的依据。例如：

英语教学活动中的情境和任务应为学生所熟悉，体现交际的真实性。因此我采用任务教学、情境教学方法，让学生在有趣、开放式的语言环境中，学会观察、思考、讨论和总结，在"用"中发展思维能力、创新意识和各种语言应用能力。小学英语课堂教学的生命就在于激发学生学习英语的兴趣，为学生提供足够的机会用英语进行活动。因此，在教学方法的总体构思上，我注重学生听、说、读、演等方面能力的综合训练，采用导学互动教学模式和多媒体辅助教学。同时在教学过程中我注重学生学习方法的指导，指导学生学习使用或学会使用学习方法，如五官并用、强化记忆、比较归纳，结合本课教学培养学生观察力、记忆力、想象力、注意力、创造力、思维能力等。因此，我采用游戏的方式进行教学，这符合新课标的要求。英语新课标倡导任务型的教学模式，让学生在教师的指导下，感知语言材料。通过猜一猜、

说一说、采访等活动,让学生在动静交错、个人与小组竞争相融合的活动中习得英语,形成积极的学习态度。

(5)说教学过程。

说教学过程是说课的重点,在此环节中要具体说明执教者是怎样安排教学过程,同时说明为什么这样安排,即设计意图是什么。一般情况下此环节具体说明内容包含: Warm-up、Presentation、Practice and Production、Summary。

① Warm-up:热身环节要设计一些趣味性强的活动,调动学生的学习积极性。热身内容要与教学内容相关,起到铺垫的作用。在说课的过程中,要说明热身活动的设计内容和理论依据。

② Presentation:此步骤中执教者要说明在教学新授内容时,要设计什么样的教学活动,为什么这样设计。如在PEP五上Unit 3 What would you like?中的Let's talk的教学中新知呈现如下:

- 创设大情境: There is a food festival at Yinzuo Square.银座广场正在举行美食节,你想去吗? OK, let's go.这时播放美食节视频《舌尖上的中国》。
- 出示美食节上的食物图片, So many delicious food, what would you like to eat?提供语言支架I'd like...引导学生回答。在这个简单的师生、生生对话中引出本对话中的生词sandwich。
- 教学sandwich,同时教学本课重点句型: What would you like to eat? I'd like some... 教师领读,师生、生生操练,熟练掌握重点句型,并板书。
- 出示饮料图片果汁可乐等, T: At the festival, there are also many tasty drinks. If you are thirsty, what would you like to drink? 在美食节上还有很多可口的饮料呢,如果你渴了,你想要喝什么呀? 教师做干渴状,教学thirsty,教学另一个重点句型: What would you like to drink? I'd like some ...师生、生生根据图片操练,教师领读并板书 to drink。

设计意图:创设语言大情境,使学生感知词汇和句型,提供图片和语言支架操练巩固重点句型。通过生生、师生之间的大量语言交流,鼓励学生大胆开口,勇于表达,逐渐让学生体会到学习英语的快乐。

③ Practice and Production: "practice"是对新授内容的巩固与内化,"production"是对学习内容巩固后的拓展与用。它们之间存在着一定的联系,又有明显的层次,先练习巩固,后拓展应用。

如在PEP五上Unit 3 What would you like?中的Let's talk的教学中设计了小调查的练习:

创设情境:美食节上有很多的外国朋友,主办方请求你帮他们做一份小调查,以帮助他们及时调整美食产品。学生四人在小组内做调查,组长和组员之间用句型: What would you like to eat? I'd like some... What would you like to drink? I'd like some ... 对话,并在表格内做选择。最后由组长汇报S1 likes to eat some .../drink some ...教师作适时引导,可以适当渗透What's your favourite food? My favourite food is ... 为B部分的内容作铺垫。这样把对话情景化、生活化,学生开口说的动力油然而生,对语言的理解更深入、透彻。

④ Summary:引导学生总结归纳,要总结哪些内容,其目的是什么,如何总结,起到什么

作用,都要在说课的过程中进行详细说明。

（6）说板书设计。

板书设计要语言精练,布局合理。可以采用思维导图、与内容相关的图形、图案等,凸显讲授的内容和教学思路,并借此启迪学生的思路。

（7）说教学反思。

如果是课后的说课,教学反思是十分必要的。下面是PEP《英语（三年级起点）》四年级上册Unit 4 My Home中的Let's learn课时教学设计的教学反思:

义务教育阶段英语课程的总体目标是培养学生初步的综合语言运用能力,并通过英语学习促进学生的心智发展,提高学生的综合人文素养。作者执教完本课后,也在问自己是否完成了英语教育赋予的教育使命。同时,也对本课的教学有着自己的理解和感悟。

① 语境铺路,学以致用。

现代外语教育应注重语言学习的过程,强调语言学习的实践性,主张学生在语境中接触、体验和理解真实语言,并在此基础上学习和运用语言。英语课程提倡采用既强调语言学习过程又有利于提高学生学习成效的语言教学途径和方法,尽可能多地为学生创造在真实语境中运用语言的机会。作者在课堂始终努力地铺设真实的情境,为学生提供一次又一次的语言操练的机会,达到学以致用的最终目的。

比如,笔者在热身环节创设了参观教师新房的情境,在导入环节创设了教师要购买家居用品的情境,在拓展环节,教师又进一步创设了要设计新房的情境,这些情境都为教学增添了活力,为学生的英语学习搭建了语言实践的平台。

② 兴趣引路,事半功倍。

义务教育阶段的英语课程应能够使学生通过学习英语和使用英语,发展语言运用能力和人际交往能力,形成积极的情感态度和有效的学习策略。积极的情感态度有利于促进学生主动学习和持续发展。它还在分级目标中明确地把二级目标的第一条列为:对英语学习有持续的兴趣和爱好。

笔者在教学中用兴趣引路,精心设计各种生动有趣的活动,调动了学生参与课堂的积极性,激发了学生学习英语的内驱力,让学生在轻松愉悦的氛围中收获了语言知识,享受了语言学习的魅力。比如,抢沙发游戏、摆餐具游戏、What is missing?游戏、TPR快速反应游戏等都给英语学习注入了快乐的元素,使学习达到了事半功倍的效果。

③ 尊重个体,另辟蹊径。

义务教育阶段的英语课程应面向全体学生。课程要体现以学生为主体的思想,在教学目标、教学内容、教学过程、教学评价和教学资源的利用与开发等方面都应考虑全体学生的发展需求,课程应成为学生在教师指导下构建知识、发展技能、拓展视野、活跃思维、展现个性的过程。英语学习在很大程度上是个性化的活动,学习者由于年龄、性格、认知方式、生活环境等方面的差异而具有不同的学习需求和学习特点。

笔者在本课教学中针对学生的个体差异和学习特点,设计了不同形式的活动,有听、有说、有猜,还有做动作、做橡皮泥家具,这些活动满足了不同学习个体的需求,在拓展环节的展示过程中,笔者鼓励学生的发散思维,力求学生的创新思维,追求语言输出的美丽风景,成就了一个个独特的个体。

④ 文化旅行,陶冶身心。

英语教育应能使学生在学习和使用英语的过程中体验英语丰富的文化内涵,特别是了解中外文化的差异,形成初步的跨文化意识和初步的跨文化交际能力。

笔者在教学中通过摆餐具游戏、选书橱活动等活动,有意渗透中西方的建筑风格差异和餐具文化差异,带学生进行了一次文化的旅行,陶冶了学生的身心,拓宽了国际视野,领略了西方文化的魅力。

三、说课稿模板及样例

1. 说课稿模板

流　　程	例　　句
开场白	1. Good morning, respected experts. It's my honor to give a presentation of my teaching plan. My topic today is _____ (课题名称) It consists of six parts. 2. Good morning, my dear judges. I'm very glad to stand here and share my teaching design. There are six parts.
Part I Analysis of the teaching material	This text introduces _____ (主题), explaining _____ (课文内容大意概况). As it is the _____ (课时数) lesson of the text, some language items and background information related to the text have been introduced. In addition, the general idea of the text has been learned through initial reading and related exercises. This lesson will focus on _____ (文本哪一部分), mainly giving an introduction to _____ (文本主题), which prepares the students for a better understanding of the whole text. The reading skill—_____ is involved in the lesson, which sets a certain foundation for students' further learning—_____.(与前后教学内容的联系)
Part II Analysis of the students	1. As Grade Four students, they have certain ability of listening, speaking, reading and writing. 2. The students have learned the new words and previewed the text beforehand. 3. With certain ability about listening, speaking, reading and writing, students have been accustomed to gaining knowledge from the different and practical teaching activities and teaching tasks. 4. They are confident and eager to show themselves. 5. They have strong desire to know more about the foreign history and culture.
Part III Teaching objectives	1. On studying the teaching material and the students, I put forward the teaching objectives from Knowledge objectives, Ability objectives and Moral objectives. 2. Based on the analysis of teaching material and students, I hope the following objectives can be achieved. 3. Knowledge objectives: All the students are able to memorize, understand and use the new words _____, and sentence pattern _____. 4. Ability objectives: Students can use some reading strategies, such as _____. What's more, by role-play, _____, they can develop their _____. 5. Moral objectives: Students get to know more about rules at home and school. They learn to behave themselves so that they can get along well with others.

（续表）

流　程	例　　句
Part IV　Teaching importance and difficulties	Centering on the teaching objectives, it is of great importance for students to use the sentence pattern _____ to express _____ in daily life. And the teaching difficulties are to pronounce the vowel sounds _____ and _____ correctly.
Part V　Teaching methods and aids	1. The TPR method is adopted in my teaching. Meanwhile, group work, free talk and role-play ensure students to study in a relaxed and agreeable atmosphere. And in this class, I will use PPT and flash cards as teaching aids. 2. In my class I will use Direct Method and Task-based Language Teaching. Pictures are my teaching aids. 3. To make it easier to learn I'll adopt the Situational Teaching Approach. Students can work independently, in pairs and in groups to solve problems. Video clips and blackboard are widely used in my class.
Part VI　Teaching procedures	Step 1: Warm-up　　　　　　Step 1: Warm up and lead-in Step 2: Presentation　　　　Step 2: Pre-reading Step 3: Practice　　　　　　Step 3: While-reading Step 4: Production　　　　　Step 4: Post-reading Step 5: Summary　　　　　　Step 5: Summary Step 6: Homework　　　　　Step 6: Homework
Blackboard design	The blackboard are divided into two parts. There are _____ on the left, and _____ on the right.
结束语	1. These are my tentative ideas of this class. There are full of various situations in class, which requires the teacher with sufficient professional knowledge and the ability to deal with the problems flexibly. That's all about my teaching plan. Thank you! 2. All the above are just my tentative ideas of this class. In fact, there are various occurrences in teaching, which requires teachers to have sufficient professional knowledge and the ability to solve the problems flexibly.

2. 说教学过程（Teaching procedures）内容样例

Part VI　Teaching procedures

样例1

On the analysis above, my teaching steps are as follows:

Step 1　Lead-in

At the very beginning of the class the following questions are presented, which are designed to motivate the students and to prepare for the further learning.

When asked the question _____, students may say _____. Then I will _____. If students can't say _____, they will be encouraged to _____.

Step 2　Fast reading

Students are allowed to go over paragraph 1−7 the fastest they can to find the answers to

questions:

　　Question one _____

　　Question two _____

This step is designed to help students get the main idea as well as to drill their reading skill—skimming. If students have some difficulties in summarizing the general idea, I will ask them to do the multiple-choice question.

Both **Step 3 and Step 4** are about the detail of the text. I will introduce language items while explaining the text. Why do I divide it into two steps? The different main idea and learning skill practised are taken into account. Paragraph 1−3 mainly concern the view that _____ Through learning the three paragraphs, students' reading skill—scanning can be practised. Paragraph 4−7 argue that _____ Listening skill—listen for the specific information can be trained.

Language items are introduced when explaining the text. They cover important phrases and proper names. Phrases include _____ Students will learn to use them by means of translation and sentence-making exercises. Proper names contain _____, which are introduced with the help of map and pictures.

The purposes of the two parts are to enrich students' linguistic knowledge and to drill students learning skills as well as to broaden their cultural view.

Step 5 is about skills training. First, students are required to look for the thesis statement while reviewing the text. Second, students are encouraged to summarize _____. They may give various answers to the question. Let them share their thoughts as many as possible if time permits. Then, the writing skill—outline is presented. Students can make an outline of the text as a practice.

This step is intended to help students better understand the text as a whole as well as develop their reading and writing skills.

Step 6　Homework

Homework 1 and 2 are required homework. Every student should finish them. Homework 3 is elective one. Students can finish it by means of speaking or writing activity.

The aim is to develop students' reading, writing and speaking ability. Meanwhile, it can prepare the students for their further study.

If time permits, I will share with the class a music video _____ at the end of the class.

样例 2

On the analysis above, my teaching procedures are Presentation, Practice, and Consolidation and Extension.

Presentation

1. Lead-in

Students watch a video clip and guess _____. Then I will make a brief introduction to the social background of the time.

A good beginning is half done. Lead-in is designed to arouse students' curiosity. Multi-media is used to stimulate students' sense system. Besides, the social background can help students understand the text better.

2. After lead-in, students listen to the text and find out the expressions they hear. Students get the main idea of the text through this step.

3. Group work: Next, students read the text carefully in groups and discuss questions. In my opinion, answering questions is a good way to get the details. At the same time, the language points are presented in the answers.

The aims are: (1) to let the students understand details of the text. (2) to develop students' cooperative spirit.

Practice

1. Students study the language points in groups. During group study, I will go into the groups to help and to check their study. If they have learned well, I will go on to the next step. If I find they have some problems, for example _____, in that case, I will explain and offer some exercises for them to practice more.

The new curriculum promotes cooperation and exploration. The purposes here are to drill language points and to develop students' autonomous learning competence.

2. Then, students finish "True or False" on the basis of understanding the details. "True or False" consists of 2 sentences which can summarize the main idea of this text. After that, students retell the text.

The purposes are: (1) to help students review and consolidate the language points and the text. (2) to help students get the skills of retelling. (3) to offer students opportunities to practice spoken English.

3. Next, students watch a video clip "_____". I'll ask students to imitate the body language.

Body language is a kind of nonverbal communication. The ability to recognize and perform it is necessary to achieve fluency in a language. The purposes of the activity are to let students experience body language and to form a consciousness of using it.

Consolidation and Extension

After the practice above, students are asked to finish one of the two activities: Talk-show or Role-play.

The reasons are: (1) to check whether students can use the language points flexibly and whether they can make use of body language. This is the teaching importance and difficulties of this class. (2) to offer students an opportunity to complete tasks in which students use language to achieve a specific outcome. The activities reflect real life and students are free to use any language they want. They can stimulate students' enthusiasm and creativity.

Homework

First, required homework. Every student should finish it. Second, elective homework. Students choose one to finish if they can.

The aim of this is to develop students' writing ability and communicative ability.

样例 3

Next let's come to the most important part—teaching procedures.

Step1　Warm up

Before class I will divide the whole class into two groups: G1 vs G2. Each group will have their own bamboo. Either group performs better, their bamboo will grow higher. At the end of the class, the group with the higher bamboo will win.

After greeting students, I will suggest a game: Let's chant. I will ask students to answer my questions and point to their parts of the body. It starts like this:

T: Where is your nose?

S: This is my nose. This is my nose.

In this way we can get all of the students involved and activate the atmosphere. What's more, we can finish the task and prepare for the listening.

Step 2　Presentation

Students look at the picture and guess the meaning of the new phrases. I'll teach like this: "Look at the girl. She is taking a handkerchief and her nose is red. Can you guess what happened to her?" It is easy for them to guess the meaning "have a cold" . Picture is a good way to present language points. By this means, students get to know the meaning of this phrase as well as others.

Then students will listen to the recorder and number the names. They will know more information about the students in the pictures.

After that I ask students to repeat after the recording. They can work in pairs to practice the conversation. The more volunteers, the better. Students in G1 show more enthusiasm and they did a much better job. So their bamboo grows higher. I will encourage students in G2 to try harder next time. Through the activities students' pronunciation and intonation will be practiced and improved.

Step 3　Pre-listening

Four students in a group discuss the question "What should they do if they have health problems?" Brainstorming will be introduced in this step, which helps students better understand the following listening task.

Step 4　While-listening

There are three tasks in the step: Number the pictures, Listen and check, Listen and finish the chart. The first two tasks are easier. Most of the students tend to finish them without difficulties. The third one is much more difficult. These teaching activities are designed to meet students' needs with different levels.

Step 5　Post-listening

With enough input students are expected to role play the conversation. I will invite some students to perform in front of the class. The students who perform better will contribute to their group.

Then students in G1 and G2 will have a debate over the topic: _____. After the debate students come to realize that it is bad to eat unhealthily.

Step 6　Summary

Students are invited to share what they have learned in this lesson. And also I will give a quick review of the key points.

Step7　Homework

1. For all of the students they have to memorize the new words and phrases and there will be a dictation next class.

2. For students who want to challenge themselves they can do an interview about their family members' health problems.

四、说课训练模拟题

抽题：

某某考生教师资格面试试题　　　抽题时间：8∶10

要求：1. 教师用全英进行说课。

2. 教师要有示范性朗读。

3. 教师的所讲内容教学目标明确,重难点突出,练习有梯度。

图书在版编目(CIP)数据

小学英语教学技能实训/朱莹主编.—上海:复旦大学出版社,2019.8(2025.1 重印)
普通高等学校小学教育专业系列教材
ISBN 978-7-309-14519-9

Ⅰ.①小…　Ⅱ.①朱…　Ⅲ.①英语课-教学法-小学-高等学校-教材　Ⅳ.①G623.312

中国版本图书馆 CIP 数据核字(2019)第 164460 号

小学英语教学技能实训
朱　莹　主编
责任编辑/查　莉

复旦大学出版社有限公司出版发行
上海市国权路 579 号　邮编:200433
网址:fupnet@fudanpress.com　http://www.fudanpress.com
门市零售:86-21-65102580　团体订购:86-21-65104505
出版部电话:86-21-65642845
常熟市华顺印刷有限公司

开本 787 毫米×1092 毫米　1/16　印张 11.75　字数 265 千字
2025 年 1 月第 1 版第 9 次印刷
印数 27 726—32 825

ISBN 978-7-309-14519-9/G·2012
定价:48.00 元